Here's the Catch

Here's the Catch

A Memoir of the Miracle Mets and More

RON SWOBODA

Thomas Dunne Books
St. Martin's Press
New York

THOMAS DUNNE BOOKS.
An imprint of St. Martin's Press.

HERE'S THE CATCH. Copyright © 2019 by Ronald Swoboda. All rights reserved. Printed in the United States of America. For information, address St. Martin's Press, 175 Fifth Avenue, New York, N.Y. 10010.

www.thomasdunnebooks.com
www.stmartins.com

The Library of Congress Cataloging-in-Publication Data is available upon request.

ISBN 978-1-250-23566-4 (hardcover)
ISBN 978-1-250-23567-1 (ebook)

Our books may be purchased in bulk for promotional, educational, or business use. Please contact your local bookseller or the Macmillan Corporate and Premium Sales Department at 1-800-221-7945, extension 5442, or by email at MacmillanSpecialMarkets@macmillan.com.

First Edition: June 2019

10 9 8 7 6 5 4 3 2 1

Contents

Acknowledgments

This book wouldn't have gotten written without the urging of my friend Rob Couhig, an attorney here in New Orleans who heard some of my baseball stories and stayed on me to write them down. And then, there's John Stinson, who worked with me in the beginning and whose fringy lifestyle belies a love and facility with words and language. Most critical was Jamie Malinowski, found for me by my able agent, David McCormick. It was Jamie who managed to see a book in the pile of writing I dumped on him. My publisher, Tom Dunne, and my editor, Stephen S. Power, paid me the highest of compliments when they bought into my quixotic journey as an author, while assistant editor Janine Barlow made sure the road was clear and easily traveled. Lastly, I can't appreciate enough the book's copy editor, Fred Chase, and its production editor, Ken Silver, who, like my mom, patiently and carefully cleaned up all my spills and put the furniture back where it belonged. And of course none of this would have been possible without my '69 Mets teammates and in particular their wives and former wives who shared their poignant memories of that season, some for the first time.

My thanks to all.

Here's the Catch

us players, frightening and fun at the same time, our focus honed sharp, ready to engrave a neural etching that we will, each of us, take to our graves.

In right field, I was ready. I'd worked hard teaching myself to get a good jump. Eddie Yost, our third base coach, was a wizard with a fungo bat—the long, light bat used in fielding drills. He would get me on the end of it, about 150 feet away, and hit me thousands of balls of all kinds, hard grounders and line drives, balls in front of me, balls over my head, to the left and right. The point of the drill was to help me make tough reads and tough plays, in the moment, with gamelike speed. I wasn't just practicing catching the ball; I was practicing seeing the ball right off the bat. Nothing will make you a better outfielder.

With the tying run at third, I'm thinking that if the ball is hard hit, I'm comfortable going back for it; but if the ball is softly hit, I will want to be in position to try and throw the runner out at the plate, so it might be better for me to move in a couple steps. In the batter's box, Brooksie has to be hunting fastball. Seaver featured mostly hard stuff, including a four-seam heater in the upper 90s, a two-seamer with hard run in on a right-handed hitter (which Robinson was), and a hard slider. Such was Seaver's command that the venerable manager Gene Mauch liked to say, "He could throw it into a teacup." Wherever Seaver decided to throw the ball, it would go there.

Watching the replay on YouTube—something utterly unfathomable in the moment—it looks like Seaver, pitching from the stretch, goes with his two-seamer down and away, hoping to induce a ground ball and maybe even an inning-ending double play. In which case, game over, we win. But Brooksie squares it up, and lines the pitch sharply toward short right center field.

I had made some incredibly embarrassing mistakes when I first came to the big leagues. I committed 11 errors as an outfielder in my rookie season, second worst in the league—what we call taking the routine out of a routine fly ball. In 1968, I made six—better, but still good for the lead among National League right fielders. When the ball is hit to someone who makes that many errors, everyone holds their breath, expecting an adventure. Exacerbating the problem was Shea Stadium, which stood three tiers tall, like a gigantic Globe Theatre. Instead of sky, most fly balls, plus all the liners and little loopers, had the grandstands as a background. With fans there in constant motion, I often felt like I was staring into an ebbing, flowing Jackson Pollock painting, amping up my indecisiveness, which is my fatal flaw, to an almost Shakespearean dimension. Years later, I saw Monet's paintings from the Marmottan Museum in Paris, and I couldn't help but wonder what Monet would have seen had he ever stood in right field at Shea and looked into that mercurial autumn light falling on the shouting, shifting fans.

Not then, though. I just broke for the ball.

Later, there was no small amount of debate over the wisdom of my pursuit of Brooksie's falling line drive. Our first baseman, Donn Clendenon, one of those outspoken, self-appointed in-house arbiters known throughout baseball as clubhouse lawyers, but who was the only one I ever heard of who actually took a law degree and passed the bar exam, was quoted as calling me "a dumb SOB for trying to catch it" because if it got by me two runs score, and we would have trailed by at least a run going into the bottom of the ninth. That's possible, but I've always maintained that Boog Powell would have had to grow wings on his heels to bring his bargelike body around from first to score. Regardless, in my moment of exquisite focus all I knew was . . . GO! Which I did. Joe Pignatano, our bullpen coach, a great friend of Hodges and the last living member of our coaching staff, once gave me a priceless piece of advice. "Swoboda," he said, "don't think. You will only hurt the team." So, I didn't. Not then. I launched into full-bore pursuit sharply to my

I am the joyful and humble beneficiary of my parents, John and Dolores Swoboda, who worked their entire lives to make it possible for me to play the game of baseball and progress to its professional pinnacle. And forever, the love of my life, my best friend and partner and, really, my hero, my wife of fifty-four years, Cecilia, who gave me two great sons, Ron Jr. and Brian, and made me one of the most fortunate souls who can say he's been loved every second of his life.

Prologue: Breaking for the Ball

It's a cool late afternoon in New York in mid-October of 1969. In the gloaming, a bunting-covered Shea Stadium, alive with the pulse of a capacity crowd, is draped in long shadows that mute colors and sharpen the edges between light and dark, success and failure. I'm in right field, in the only World Series I will ever see from the inside. My overachieving New York Mets, perennial laughingstocks of the National Pastime, lead the rightly favored Baltimore Orioles two games to one, and we are nursing a one–nothing lead in the top of the ninth inning of Game Four. Our right-handed ace George Thomas Seaver—"Tom Terrific," "The Franchise"—has been moving through the Orioles' batting order as unstoppably as the earth around the sun, all part of his inexorable journey to the Hall of Fame. Three seasons in the pros, he's already accumulated 57 career wins, and a Cy Young Award is about to elbow its way onto his mantel. But at this moment, after eight innings of excellence, he is in trouble. With one out, back-to-back base hits by Frank Robinson, the O's future Hall of Fame outfielder and two-time MVP, and Boog Powell, their slugging first baseman, have put runners at first and third. Brooks Robinson, the O's shoo-in Hall of Fame third baseman, is at the plate. Our manager, Gil Hodges, who starred at first base for the Brooklyn Dodgers in the 1950s and who played in seven World Series, more than anybody in either dugout, has one of the most able brains in baseball. In this pregnant moment, the tall, lean Indianan, his royal blue warmup jacket buttoned to the neck, takes a slow walk to the mound to make sure the infielders and everyone else are on the same page. He has our top relievers, Ron Taylor and Tug McGraw, warming in the bullpen. Today a manager in this predicament would almost certainly bring one of them in to close the game. (Hell, today a manager would never be in Gil's predicament, because a closer would have started the inning, and Seaver would be in the dugout cheering him on.) But in that long-gone era, an elite pitcher like Seaver is expected to finish at least half his starts. Tom is our leader, the best we have, our rock. He isn't coming out.

What had to be dawning on most folks watching was that this game and this World Series had reached its tipping point. If the Orioles seized this moment, they would tie the Series and recapture the momentum; they would have come from behind to beat Seaver at his best, and they would play two of the next three in their home park. On the other hand, if we stopped the rally and won the game, we would be holding a 3–1 lead with a chance to wrap it up at home. And at that time, only three teams in baseball's lengthy history had come back to win after a 3–1 disadvantage.

For the players, our families, and the fans, all our dreams were teetering on the fulcrum of this delicious moment. If things fall the right way, you've taken a giant leap toward a gold ring and a place in history. Things go badly and you join the long list of forgettable also-rans. We had a pair of great broadcasters working the series in NBC's Curt Gowdy and, from the Mets' broadcast team, Lindsey Nelson. Like all of us, they had to know that the universe of possibility was presenting them with situations worthy of their kinetic art, the ability both possessed to create beautiful word pictures that seem to paint themselves. What an extraordinary place to be for right with the rapidly rising fear that I wasn't going to get there on time. In my slo-mo memory, that dread seems to last a long time. If that counts as a thought, it was too late to stop.

In his grand novel, *Underworld,* the author Don DeLillo tells us about Cotter Martin, an ungainly young black kid leaping over a turnstile at the Polo Grounds in 1951, and gate-crashing the game where the New York Giants' Bobby Thomson hit the game-winning home run to beat the Brooklyn Dodgers for the National League Pennant. "He is just a running boy, a half seen figure from the streets, but the way running reveals some clue to being, the way a runner bares himself to consciousness, this is how the dark-skinned kid seems to open to the world, how the blood rush of a dozen strides brings him into eloquence." On my more fevered run, I was a young man already in his middle twenties, but like Cotter Martin, I was fully committed in a mad dash down a path that would change my life forever.

1

A Pretty Lucky Man

Grandad, why is everything always a story?" This quote comes straight from Kaylin, my now-seventeen-year-old granddaughter. She's a swimmer, and like all her classmates and buddies, she is hardly ever out of eye contact with her smartphone texting in a world that moves way faster than mine. To her soon to be seventy-five-year-old grandfather, everything *is* a story. That's how I remember everything.

I consider myself a pretty lucky man. I've been married to Cecilia, the most amazing of female creatures for fifty-four years. We have two grown sons, and their families color our charmed lives in forever surprising ways. With zero preparation, I've been able to work most of my adult life in a job that most people would love to have, working in TV sports as an anchor and a reporter. Not bad for a guy with a flat average IQ. Most people know me, if they know me at all, for the nine years I played Major League Baseball, mostly for the New York Mets, including the Miracle Mets team that won the 1969 World Championship, but also with the New York Yankees, and briefly with the Expos and Braves in the spring of 1974. A study in the August 2007 issue of *Population Research and Policy Review* looked at the 5,989 position players who began their careers between 1902 and 1993—that would include me—and found that the average length of a major league player's career during that time was 5.6 years. With nine years' service, I was a journeyman who beat the odds. If there is one characteristic that ties all those experiences together, it's that almost all of my life has been spent around people more capable and more disciplined than myself, all to my benefit. As I say, I'm a pretty lucky man.

Three things happened to me as a kid that could have changed everything. Once, riding my bike when I was about five in the neighborhood where I grew up, Sparrows Point, Maryland, I came out of a blind alleyway just five feet ahead of a point where I would have meshed with the grille of a Buick Roadmaster.

Later, when I was about fourteen years old, a couple buddies and I were destroying the inside of this abandoned house, you know, busting out the windows, tearing up anything we could. But climbing down off the roof required dangling your legs from an overhang and placing your feet on the rungs of a ladder you couldn't see and could barely feel with your toes extended. Well, my feet went through the rungs and I fell backward onto the ladder from about ten feet high. Fortunately, and totally accidentally, I hooked a rung of the ladder with my knees flexed, breaking my fall. My momentum pulled the ladder from the house down on top of me, and I landed in a shaken but safe heap on the ground.

A few years later, when I was older but not wiser, I took my Daisy Pump BB gun into the piece of woods that stood right across the street from where I lived. I considered myself the scourge of the starling and grackle population around my yard. I hunted them hard, sitting quietly below the mulberry trees where they came to feed. Some neighborhood guys, however, wanted to up the stakes, and proposed a BB gunfight. Diving into sides, we squared off in the woods about 150 feet apart. We'd pop up and shoot at the other guys with only a rough idea of who we were shooting at. Smart, no? You know where this is heading. At some point during the fray, a

BB hit me in the forehead about an inch and a half above my right eye, which is what it took for me to grasp the stupidity of what we were doing. So, I ran home, never to do that again.

It is only looking back that you understand, with complete clarity, that any one of these three things could have changed my life completely. It was just luck. I do not believe there are angels lurking about saving kids ready to fall to their deaths from high places, or ride their bikes in front of cars, or take a BB in the eye. It was luck, and all the stories that follow have depended on nothing but luck.

Growing Up

I grew up in Maryland in a community called Sparrows Point outside Baltimore, hard by a Bethlehem Steel plant, once the first and largest integrated tidewater steel manufacturing plant in America. Sparrows Point is tidewater because it's located on a stretch of land where the Chesapeake Bay gives way to the Patapsco River, which carries oceangoing ships to and from the port of Baltimore, four or five miles to the north. The deep water access allowed the plant to receive by boat the first iron ore from outside the continental USA, specifically, from Cuba, following the Spanish-American War. We'd see those huge vessels coming up to Bethlehem Steel, a massive operation that came into being around the turn of the twentieth century and that, at its peak, produced 610,000 tons of steel and employed 35,000 people round-the-clock. Now, after more than a hundred springs, it's all gone, and the property is being repurposed.

I was the younger of two boys: a rambunctious, inquisitive kid. My neighborhood was best described as the scruffy suburbs, where the lady with the perfect perm and meticulously tended rosebushes could live next door to a shirtless guy who had an old Ford sitting on cinder blocks in his backyard. We had one, thanks to my older brother, Jack. But it was the kind of place where you felt completely secure, safe riding your bike to school or the playground. During the hot months, we went to what we called summer school, where a teacher operated a day camp with crafts and softball games. Early evenings were dedicated to Little League. Once we learned to swim, we were on our own, at all the available swimming sites in Back River. Everybody knew one another. It was idyllic—a perfect upbringing.

My Mom and Dad were working people. They bought a house on Lakeview Avenue that they lived in most of their lives until it burned down years later when my son was living in the upstairs apartment. We didn't live in luxury, but we never lacked for love or the sense that our parents cared for us, although they surely expected us to be responsible for our end of the deal. Between my parents and my wife, Cecilia, I know that I've been loved every day of my life. No small statement. For years my Mom could walk across the dual highway at the top of our street to her work as a secretary at Arcrods Corporation. They manufactured welding rods, coated with asbestos, likely the source of the mesothelioma my Mom was diagnosed with after her retirement. Mom had an artistic streak and loved to arrange flowers. She actually studied it and tried to work for a florist, but the pressure to perform was too much at her age. She also made an excellent crab soup, the Maryland staple. My Dad had been a waist-gunner on a B-29 stationed on Tinian, in the Marianas, during the last five months of the war. When he came back to civilian life, he sold insurance, worked as an automobile mechanic, then a service salesman, and, eventually, a service manager at several auto dealerships in Baltimore. After taking some night courses, he took his last and most fulfilling job, as an auto-mechanics teacher at Eastern Vo-Tech High School in the nearby community of Dundalk.

Jack, my only sibling, was born thirteen months before me, and we were opposites in just about every way possible. Jack liked a little danger; I did not. If you pissed him off, he might take you on a tour of fist city; I resisted that sort of confrontation. Jack had a small physical frame; I would grow to just over six feet and broad-shouldered. He would take great care making plastic models of custom cars with beautiful paint jobs. (I still have one of his creations.) I would throw together the plastic models of ships and airplanes and take them behind our house and shoot them up with my BB gun. When we were kids, I never messed with him. He scared the hell out of me. But then, one day, around the age of twelve or thirteen, we were hanging out with some neighborhood kids in the woods across from our house. I don't recall what started it, but Jack and I tangled. By then I was as big or slightly bigger than he was, and this time I didn't give in or run away. Part wrestling, part fist-fighting, I stayed at it until Jack called off the jam. I don't know what it meant to him. To me, it was a rite of passage.

In high school at Sparrows Point, Jack played lacrosse, and I played baseball. In Baltimore County, they were both spring sports season, so I only got to see him play once. He was crease attack and feisty as hell. I remember he spent some time in the penalty box for using his stick more as a weapon. He loved to beat the crap out of people.

My Chinese Granddad

I had a fairly typical upbringing, which is to say, like everybody, there were elements that were unique. Mom's mother, Agnes, was a tall handsome brunette, a divorcée who liked her men. For years she worked as a waitress in a Chinese restaurant and in 1949 married one of the cooks. That's how Arthur Wong completed his journey from Canton, China, to our family in Sparrows Point. (Ironically, just a couple miles north on the Patapsco River from Sparrows Point is a Baltimore neighborhood called Canton. With just a slight adjustment in his trajectory, Arthur could have gone halfway around the world and still have never left Canton.)

Not everybody was thrilled with the marriage. Arthur was younger than Agnes and had never been married, which triggered Mom's alarms. She thought he was a playboy. But when Agnes floated the idea of the marriage past her son, my Uncle John Cramblitt, she got a different reaction. John was eighteen at the time, into motorcycles and hot rods, and engaged to a woman named Sue, who became one of my very favorite aunts. "If that's what makes her happy, it's good," he pronounced. "She has spent half her life with some miserable people."

And it was true. Agnes had experienced the male animal, but had yet to make any good choices, until she went with Arthur to the justice of the peace. Mom called Dad: "Guess what your mother-in-law just did?" "What?" Mom, aghast, "She married a Chinaman."

"She's old enough to know better," summed up Dad's feelings. That was the inauspicious beginning of the marriage that lasted the rest of their lives. I was confused with a Chinaman in the family whom I was told to call Uncle Arthur. That worked fine until I was old enough to wonder, "How can he be my uncle if he's married to my grandmother?" Kids never got the complete explanation of anything.

He had another name, An King Ben, and the suggestion that he came to America through New York under that moniker at the age of fourteen with his father. His Chinese friends called him Wong Fuk. He served in the U.S. Army, which led to his citizenship. All we really knew was that suddenly we were eating a lot of Chinese food. He showed me how to use chopsticks before I was twelve, and to this day I only eat Chinese food with chopsticks. We loved to visit

Frank Chu's restaurant, where Arthur met Agnes. Plucked chickens soon to be in the moo goo gai pan and chunks of roast pork hung in a screened-in enclosure above the prep tables. When my brother, Jack, and I walked into the kitchen, Mr. Chu grinned, calling, "Oh, Jackie-Ronnie, good to see you!" We made his day. He never forgot us. Mr. Chu imported a Chinese wife. She wanted to be called Doctor, because she claimed to be a midwife. We called her the Dragon Lady behind her back. She informed us kids at dinner that in China it was good manners to slurp your soup and burp loudly. Mom said, "Save that for when you visit China." Uncle Arthur treated Grandma Wong like a queen, and our family learned to love him as he evolved into Grandpop Wong.

After working his ass off for other people, he opened his own Cantonese restaurants in Maryland: one that failed in Silver Spring in the suburbs north of Washington, D.C., and a carry-out shop in Turner Station, a black neighborhood not far from my home. I helped him run the register and take orders. I watched him work the Chinese stove where everything was cooked in a wok. I didn't care for egg foo yung, but I liked watching him make it. He'd grab three eggs in one hand, breaking them one at a time into a sauce pan, scooping in diced onion and pork, for exactly the right number of patties cooked in hot oil. Then, as he cleaned out the wok and got ready for the next dish, he passed me the carton of egg foo yung. He did all of this while smoking a Viceroy cigarette with an extended ash that defied gravity. Today, where we live in New Orleans, there is a small Chinese restaurant that makes several Cantonese dishes, including egg roll and pork fried rice exactly the way Grandpop Wong made them.

He was a marvel at multitasking whose dexterity should have enabled him to drive a Ferrari at Le Mans. But he was the worst driver to hit the road. Uncle John Cramblitt fixed Grandpop up with a mid-sized Pontiac. It accumulated scrapes and dents like Pig-Pen accumulated dirt. Grandpop's story was that he was always getting hit by somebody in the parking lot. Unfortunately, there were witnesses. My cousin Steve was a passenger one time with Grandpop at the wheel. Steve called it the most frightening time of his life, including his hitch as an MP in Vietnam. Red lights meant nothing to Grandpop. I don't know if he was color-blind.

At the stove, Grandpop always sipped from a small glass. He said it was tea. His tea turned out to be VO. Maybe he was boxed when he left work. Outside the restaurant, Uncle John asked if he was okay to get behind the wheel. Grandpop said, "I drive like snake in grass." He backed squarely into the side of a car and pulled off down the road, never looking back. How he avoided a fatal wreck, killing himself or some innocent soul, is a miracle.

Grandpop was a city boy who preferred running with his Chinese buddies, playing mahjong, and gambling. When he came up to the woods I'd bought in Maryland with my World Series share, seventy acres of black, white, and red oaks, he was terrified. He swore that there were tigers lurking in the quiet woods, a lesson from his boyhood in China. He called them "cotton foots" because they walked so softly. You couldn't make him believe there weren't tigers. We had white-tailed deer but no cotton foots. It brings to mind that wacky scene in *Apocalypse Now,* the tiger chasing the saucier through the jungle: it's the cook, in danger of becoming a meal, who escapes the tiger.

Agnes grew up on a tobacco farm in Annapolis. (Irony: cigarettes, cigars, snuff, chewing tobacco . . . I hated the stuff.) In her mid-seventies, with Grandpop Wong cowering at the campsite, Grandma would hike through the woods alone, up and down the steep trails that crisscrossed the property. She lived into her late eighties, outlasting her husband by a dozen years.

Mom and Agnes collected Chinese art, watercolors, vases, painted porcelain figures, and wood carvings of Shou Lao, the God of Longevity—things I still have.

According to Grandpop Wong, the usual fate of Chinese cooks in America was to stand in front of a stove until their legs gave way. When they could no longer work, they were put in a room to die. Our family saved my Grandpop from that end, and he more than returned the favor. He brought a new world into our white-bread American family. And that occurred because Agnes was a liberated woman, before they invented the phrase.

Babe Ruth was a Baltimore boy who wore the Yankee pinstripes and played right field. So was I. Near the end of my two and a half seasons with the Yankees, struggling to find something that worked, I ordered a half dozen R43 bats, Ruth's model. Grandpop Wong had seen the Babe play in the original Yankee Stadium. He came to my games and loved to tell me, "You hit the ball like Baby Ruth." Once in a great while it was true.

Uncles at the Morgue

Grandpop Wong was the wild card on my mother's side; my uncles played that role on my Dad's.

My Dad grew up with three brothers and two sisters near Lexington Market, an open-air fresh food market in downtown Baltimore. My brother, Jack, and I heard Aunt Frances dying from lung cancer in the days before they quieted that up with drugs. She was in bed moaning her way out of the world. That scared the crap out of us kids. At ten years old, I had no concept of death. That changed during the funeral. She was in an open casket, and I kept thinking how uncomfortably quiet she looked lying there with a soft, shiny pillow under her head. I went to bed with that thought, and it troubled my sleep.

Dad's oldest brother, Robert, a welder and union shop steward at the Bethlehem Steel plant, lived across the street from us. For some reason, or reasons, I was never comfortable around the fellow. Dad had to remind him not to walk into our house without knocking. His son flashed my mother from his bedroom window. Do people who make you uncomfortable feel uncomfortable around people? I suppose they do.

Uncle George was the youngest of the brothers. His past could have included anything, and I do mean anything. He dropped out of school to run with Baltimore street gangs. Dishonorably discharged from the army, he worked at the city morgue. He was never mentally the sharpest knife in the drawer, but Uncle George had manliness about him, authenticity. He came at you directly. What came out of his mouth never sounded like bullshit. When Jack and I were fifteen or sixteen, Uncle George was the first grown-up to tell us dirty jokes and make us feel like we were close to being in the adult club. When he saw us with girls around, he asked me if we were hosing them. Hosing? I'd never heard it put that way. He cleared it up with *fucking*. Jack's answer was silence. Mine was,"No!"

The fascinating uncle was Bill. Laboring outdoors for the Baltimore Parks Department and getting fried in the sun, he read in the *Sunpaper* about a job opening at the morgue. He took the test, passed, and for eighteen years worked as a diener with Uncle George. They apprenticed driving the wagon, scooping stiffs. They handled and cleaned up the bodies, preparing them for autopsies. In time, they did the scalpel work, opening up chests and sawing the tops off skulls for craniotomies. When I visited, they lightened up the gruesome scene with jokes. Uncle Bill talked about dieners cutting open bodies with one hand while eating sandwiches with the other.

I don't think he was one of them, but who knows? It was an odd lot employed in the place. One man they always talked about, Mumford, who got his job through political patronage, never learned to read. At a murder scene, Uncle Bill called a detective by his first name. "It's Inspector to you." The cop was a neighborhood crony of Mumford, who strolled in, slapped the guy upside his head, and said, "Hey, Dirtyneck, what's going on?"

The morgue building was a gloomy industrial structure right on the harbor in downtown Baltimore. It sat somewhere astride death and gallows humor. On a Saturday afternoon, Jack and I would "visit the stiffs" to see what had been collected on a Friday night in Charm City. The drill was to call the morgue to find out if our uncles were there and if anything on display was worth the ride from Sparrows Point. They would mess with us. A dead guy lying in a tray with a lit cigarette in his mouth, and my Uncle Bill saying, "I told you smoking wasn't any good for you." Neither was getting shot in the face. Uncle Bill, clipboard and pen in hand, addressed a body with a 2×4 sticking out of its chest, "When were you first aware of the pain, sir?" Sick, surreal, perfect for teenage boys.

Jack knew I had a weak stomach. I could only take the macabre up to a point. He'd always offer to stop at Gino's for a hamburger, but not because he thought I might be hungry. Gino's was named for Gino Marchetti, the great defensive end for the Colts, and a fast-food pioneer. We loved the food, but Jack knew that after a couple of autopsies a medium rare cheeseburger with catsup could no longer be considered food. Nothing in the morgue experience made me want to follow forensics for a living.

For someone sadly under-schooled, Uncle Bill had a sharp mind. He gained a seat-of-the-pants education in forensic pathology. I'm told that cops and, once in a while his boss, the coroner, valued Uncle Bill's opinion when a cause of death wasn't clear. The morgue fed right into his professional sense of comedy. He told me about a suicide who had stretched himself across the railroad tracks. The train wheels divided him at the belt line. A state trooper, standing at the head of the tray, needed the dead man's statistics for his report, so he asked the diener, "Race?" "Caucasian." "Color of hair?" "Brown." "Approximate weight?" "About 155 pounds." "Approximate height?" The diener, grabbing hold of the corpse's shoes, dragged the stiff apart, its guts falling into the tray. "How tall would you like him?" The cop, puking through his fingers, swore at the morgue attendant, "You hump, if I ever catch you on the highway, I will shoot you."

On a night shift, if it got slow, the menace was medical alcohol mixed with Cokes. It wasted you fast. A wagon driver got good and stiff on it and passed out on the lawn in front of the building. Uncle Bill took a phone call from the neighborhood, inquiring if they had dropped a body on the way in. Uncle George spiked the punch bowl at a family party. People who didn't drink, and didn't think they were drinking, turned into a room full of Crazy Guggenheims.

One day when I was a teenager, my grandmother Agnes Wong came to one of my Leone's Boys Club baseball games at Swan Park. She'd sprained her ankle coming in. At the end of the game it was too swollen to walk. Uncle Bill and Uncle George carried her away in her lawn chair, both of them giggling. Grandma Wong asked what was so funny. Uncle Bill said, "This is the first time we've picked up anyone who was still alive."

Clientele checking into the morgue had no use for the clothing they arrived in. My uncles had no compunction repurposing the apparel. For three years in high school, I wore a brown corduroy car coat, a gift from Uncle Bill. Uncle George found a nice pair of dress boots on a man who met his end in a car wreck. In a bar near the morgue, Uncle George was talking about this unlucky soul. "I'd hate to be in his shoes," someone said. Uncle George added, "It ain't as bad you think."

At family gatherings, Uncle Bill stationed himself at the kitchen table. We'd feed him beers, and he supplied the jokes all night long. Everything in the conversation reminded him of another one-liner or a funny story. You couldn't tell him a joke he hadn't heard. It was performance. Sitting next to Dad at the Moose Club, Uncle George listened with a slow burn to a guy ragging my Dad about his bald head. When he'd heard enough, Uncle George reached across the table and grabbed the Moose by his tie, so he could use it as a lever for a series of left jabs. Not a new move for my uncle. This time a clip-on tie snapped off in Uncle George's hand. The table cracked up, including Uncle George and the Moose, who never knew how close he came to eating a knuckle sandwich.

Morgue life ended for both uncles. Never far from a can of beer, drinking in the morning when he got up until he shut it down at night, Uncle George died of cancer years after doctors removed his larynx. Uncle Bill, well into his second marriage to a disagreeable woman, blew his brains out with a .38 pistol one evening in the basement of his home. The wagon came and took him to the new morgue building where he had worked only a couple of years, before being dismissed.

The Nice Guy

One man who had a tremendous impact on me was our next-door neighbor named John Rider. He worked as a night watchman at the Bethlehem Steel Plant, and he was the law. Behind his house he tended a half-acre flower and vegetable garden, a pigeon coop, and two frog ponds with a family of Maryland snapping turtles that fed on the frogs. Rising eight feet from the strip of ground between the ponds was a triple-decker birdhouse, home to the purple martins when they flew up from the south. John Rider was what I thought of as a naturalist. He'd take me fishing in Back River and fill the boat with white perch. He made baskets from the shells of his snapping turtles. Once, after he dispatched a turtle to make soup, he cut the heart out and put it in my hands, still beating. What a constitution.

John Rider is what I refer to as a closet nice guy. His gruffness said, Don't tread on me, and I never did. I could hit all the baseballs I wanted over the fence into his garden. If I kept to the garden paths and remembered to close the gate, I had nothing to fear from John Rider.

Joe Clark, a kid from up the road, didn't get it. He decided he needed to explore John Rider's garden world. I warned him, be careful. Joe wasn't the careful type. When he hoisted up one of John Rider's bullfrogs and waved it in the air, I told him he'd better stop. He persisted. Suddenly out of the back of the house jogs John Rider. The next thing I see is him grabbing Joe by the back of the neck and kicking him in the ass as he crab-walked him out of the garden.

The first time I talked to John Rider, he told me with a straight face that when he was growing up, if kids were no good they were taken out back and shot. I believed every word. And he had guns, lots of guns. He wouldn't have to worry about me. We had a wonderful, enduring relationship. Summer evenings after I'd played baseball all day, I'd ride home on my bike, glove strung to the handlebars. If he was sitting on the bench by the ponds, I'd park my bike, say hello, and sit talking with him. He seemed to know everything I wanted to learn about nature. I bombed him with questions.

He was the guardian of the songbirds. He sat on the bench with his Winchester pump action rifle under his leg, loaded with .22 birdshot. He'd quit using bullets after an unfortunate ricochet off the birdhouse pole clipped him in the chest. When nuisance birds like English starlings came around to bother the purple martins, robins, and certain sparrows, John Rider would deal with them.

His workshop was in a long shed on the back of his house, and it was an amazing place, full of guns and tools, where he made his birdhouses and the turtle baskets. He lacquered the shells to preserve them and fashioned handles out of the turtles' breastplates. The baskets held nuts and nails. It didn't occur to me that in my lifetime I would ever make as good use of my hands as John Rider.

John Rider was still living when I left to attend the University of Maryland in the fall of 1962. On breaks from school, I'd find him by the ponds. When I left to play professional baseball a year and a half later, I got word he had died. His house and property sold. The frog ponds were filled in. There was no more garden, no more pigeons, no more purple martins. Dad lived next door until his passing on April 22, 2018. A couple years ago I saw a snapping turtle burrowing into the bank of a stream running along the back edge of the property to build a nest. I enjoy thinking that maybe there is a piece of John Rider still left in that place.

Baseball

The constant was baseball.

At nine I was in a cap-and-T-shirt league in Edgemere. Everybody seemed better than me. At thirteen, I played at Lynch Point on a small diamond with Richie Golph, tall and loose, called "Slimy Ligaments," and one-armed Frank Knorr. There wasn't enough grass on the field to tell the difference between infield and outfield. When the equipment was unpacked, the catching gear had a peculiar odor that, in the way your olfactory holds the oldest memories, has stayed with me the rest of my life. Amongst these guys I was just another kid trying to play ball, nothing special at all at that time.

At fourteen going on fifteen, Charlie Butts, the father of Larry Butts, a classmate at Sparrows Point, who is still a good old friend of mine, took us to a tryout with the Gordon Stores squad, the best fourteen to sixteen age group team in Baltimore City. The tryout was on an invitation-only basis from the coach, Sterling "Sheriff" Fowble. He had coached Al Kaline, who at age eighteen left Southern High School in Baltimore for a Hall of Fame career with the Detroit Tigers. Larry, a left-handed pitcher, made the team and I landed the last contract Sheriff gave out and played third behind Dave Pivac, who went on to play football at Notre Dame and with the Los Angeles Rams. We played four or five days a week in different leagues in and around Baltimore. We were good, but we never got as far as the title game in the Cardinal Gibbons Tournament, the city championships, which was played at Memorial Stadium, then the home of the Baltimore Orioles.

The next season, Sheriff Fowble moved me to the outfield, an indignity at the time, like being cast out of the Garden of Eden, but it was the best thing that could have happened in the long run. My first game in left, I ran down a ball hit over my head and fired it back in to the relay man, who threw the hitter out at third base. Not bad. It was still baseball out there, and I came to love it. We won the Cardinal Gibbons Tournament that year and although I wasn't the star, I hit a home run in Memorial Stadium just over the fence down the left field line. If I were scouting myself, I would say I had some power and was developing a good arm. But dreams of playing in the big leagues were just that—dreams!

The next summer, after my senior year in high school, I played for the Dolphin club. I was in the lineup every day, but learned nothing. The upshot was landing a workship at the University of Maryland, which is the same as an athletic scholarship, except you had to work, cleaning the floors in a four-story dorm. I was the first college man in my family. At Maryland, I played freshman ball, studied, and cleaned the dorm to pay for my room and board. Nice work if you can get it.

I technically majored in physical education, but I was actually majoring in baseball with a minor in phys ed. And frankly, I couldn't have cared less about phys ed, but it had its benefits, particularly the gymnastics workouts, which immeasurably helped to improve my strength and overall conditioning. Being a phys ed major also had some odd requirements, one of which was a ballroom dance course. We took it for credit; the girls in the class took it noncredit because, we assumed, they wanted to meet us jocks. I had not gone to school looking for a girlfriend or a wife, just to play ball and see where that led me. But before the class could even be called to order, there was this burst of flaming red hair and a smile that made me wish with all my heart that it was for me. That was Cecilia. She just lit up the room.

Later, in the spring, when I was on the field with the U of M freshman baseball team, I noticed her in the stands. Hell, with that screaming riot of red hair, Stevie Wonder would have noticed her in the stands. Then, one Sunday morning, through some magic of happenstance or kismet, we ran into each other. We lived in the same dorm complex and took the same path to church. On this particular morning it was raining, and I had an umbrella or vice versa. So, if it was happenstance, it was the most pleasing happenstance of my life. The whole world seemed to brighten up when I spent time with her; she was just so authentically, wonderfully enthusiastic. We started dating, which was more like going for a burger now and then. She was an English major, exactly what I wasn't looking for, which, of course, turned into the best thing that ever happened to me.

After the end of the following semester, when I left for Florida to start my professional career, Cecilia tied a bundle of Doublemint Chewing Gum, a favorite of mine, to the door handle of my car. As anybody who has ever been in love knows, it's those small gestures that show a person cares for you. She made it clear.

So we wrote letters and did all we could to stay in touch. When I was playing in Williamsport, Pennsylvania, Cecilia came with my parents for a visit. When she said, "I want what you want," it was the most exciting sentence I had ever heard. And so it happened.

The summer after my freshman year was my last as an amateur, and I spent it playing for the Leone's Boys Club team, coached by the late Walter Youse, a grumpy old baseball lifer who also scouted for the Baltimore Orioles. Walter was the real deal; before Youse was through, he could boast of having coached a Hall of Famer named Reggie Jackson, Twins pitcher Dave Boswell, a bunch of us who played in the majors, and dozens more who had creditable careers in college or the minor leagues. It was a great summer, playing games every day and twice on Sunday. For Walter, you played like a pro and were expected to act like a pro. He helped you find out the two most important things: (1) did you *want* to play, and (2) *could* you play? There were no breaks to go on vacation with your folks. You signed up for the duration, and that amounted to more than ninety games.

The culmination of the summer with Walter Youse and Leone's was our trip to Johnstown, Pennsylvania, and the AAABA tournament. It was played against teams from all over America, including an all-star team from New Orleans, coached by Rags Scheuermann, the Walter Youse of the Crescent City, whom I would come to know and respect when I arrived in New Orleans as a TV guy in 1981. Rags's son, Joey, played at Tulane. I always said he looked like coaching material, especially with a bat in his hand at home plate. Today Joey walks in his Dad's shadow, coaching the Delgado

Community College team and the New Orleans All American team in the summer. He still takes that squad to Johnstown.

I had a great tournament, knocking two or three balls out of Point Stadium on our way to the finals, where we lost to the Brooklyn Cadets. When I wasn't awarded the MVP, Walter marched us off the field. Now I'm in the AAABA Hall of Fame, inducted in 1998 alongside my manager, Walter Youse.

There was a lot of talk that I was going to get a contract offer from the Orioles. That seemed to make sense—Baltimore boy? Walter Youse discovery? But it didn't quite work out that way. The Orioles splurged and gave a $70,000 bonus to a right-handed pitcher named Wally Bunker. Bunker played only nine seasons before arm trouble ended his career, but the Orioles can't say that they wasted their money. He won 19 games in 1964, and in Game Three of the 1966 World Series outdueled Claude Osteen and beat the Dodgers 1–0.

Having emptied the vault for Bunker, the O's passed not only on me but on another top prospect from Maryland: Dave Boswell. They never made me an offer. Fine, I said, I'll go back to school. Then the Mets popped up and offered me $35,000. Take it or leave it. I signed.

To say the Mets were a bad team is an enormous understatement of the word "bad." An expansion team, they played their first season in 1962 and finished in tenth and last place. The team went 40–120, setting the still current major league record for losses, with this thought: if it hadn't been for two rainouts, they could have been worse. One expects expansion teams to be bad, but the other expansion team that year, the Houston Colt 45's, had a record of 64–96, and finished eighth. Respectability was possible, but not for the Mets. They settled into last place like it was a rent-controlled apartment, and didn't give it up for years. During one of those years in the 1960s when the Dodgers were racking up titles, their star pitchers Sandy Koufax and Don Drysdale showed up on a variety show in their classy white-and-blue uniforms. When Milton Berle came out in a Mets uniform, paunchy and saggy and hopelessly unathletic, he got a huge laugh.

In my rookie year, 1965, I met Uncle Miltie in Dodger Stadium, in the ground level seats where the celebs could look right in our dugout.

2

Saboda

Swoboda. Swa-BOE-da. It means freedom or liberty in Polish. It's not that hard to pronounce, but Casey Stengel never called me anything but Saboda. No "w," not ever. Opening Day at Shea Stadium, 1965, my rookie year, my first day in the big leagues, and I was sitting on the Mets' bench versus the Los Angeles Dodgers, a sellout, 56,000 fans and me with the best seat in the house. I was twenty years old. Sweet. Nobody expected me to play. None of my family were in the stands. The hard-throwing Don Drysdale was pitching for the Dodgers: six foot six with a nasty three-quarters arm delivery that chilled right-handed hitters. Drysdale was a veteran of the Dodger-Giants knockdown wars of the 1950s, during the days of Don Newcombe and Sal "the Barber" Maglie, before hitters wore helmets. Now he had fully blossomed as an impact, front-of-the-rotation pitcher who had already accumulated 141 wins on his way to the Hall of Fame. But he wasn't my problem, at least not until the seventh inning. We were trailing. Casey seemed to be looking for someone. A pinch hitter. I tried to make myself harder to find, leaning back into the seat cushion. I really didn't think I was ready for the likes of Drysdale.

"Saboda . . . get a bat!" Casey barked in that gravel-pit voice. What could I say? "No thanks, Casey, I'd rather not." I don't think so.

I grabbed my helmet and my R-43 model Louisville Slugger from the bat rack. The "R" stands for Ruth, Babe Ruth. Up I walked to home plate, hoping to look like someone with a clue, trying to be cool. Ellis Marsalis, the sublime New Orleans pianist, father of four world-class musicians, said to me once, "When things are cool, everybody is cool." I wasn't cool, and I just hoped I wasn't visibly shaking. Tense? If someone had slapped me, I would have shattered like a rose dipped in liquid nitrogen.

First pitch, a fastball, like a really fast ball, burst into the catcher's mitt, and the umpire called "Strike one." I realized I never saw it, but it sounded like a strike. Drysdale reared, let go another blazer and I swung and missed, tardy by half a second, no idea where it was. It occurred to me the only good news here was that it didn't look like it would take long. Drysdale delivered again . . . for some reason a polite slider out over the plate that I could actually see, and better, I ripped it on a line to the second baseman. It remains the best out I ever made in baseball. Hey man, I just hit a bullet in my first at bat in the majors off Don Drysdale. You can have the out.

Pathway to the Majors

If you were surprised to read that in 1965 I was a twenty-year-old rookie major leaguer, I would understand completely. I was kind of surprised myself.

In 1964 I was invited to early spring training at the Mets major league facility in St. Petersburg, where I guess I did well enough to get myself invited to a week or so of regular spring training with the veterans on the squad, and where it became obvious I needed to be sent to Dunedin, Florida, to join the camp of the AAA Buffalo Bisons. Three weeks into the Bisons' regular season, I was sent to AA, the Eastern League in Williamsport, Pennsylvania.

I drove my 1964 Ford 390 XL Convertible, burgundy with a black top, on all local roads from Buffalo to Williamsport. The manager there was Ernie White, a former left-handed pitcher for the St. Louis Cardinals and Boston Braves for seven big league seasons in the 1940s. Ernie's job was to write my name in the lineup and, occasionally, deal with the immaturities of a nineteen-year-old athlete. Which he did with a calm and steady hand. I felt like I had a solid, productive season hitting just under .280 with 14 home runs.

Being about as naive as one could be in the company of veteran professional players, men from many backgrounds and all walks of life left me wide open. One day early during spring training with the Bisons, I was played by a Venezuelan shortstop named Elio Chacon. Elio had spent parts of three years in the big leagues, had his own baseball card and everything. So when I saw him standing next to an old Jaguar two-seater, I believed it was his. The keys were in the car and he asked me if I wanted to take it for a spin. Our workout was over, so, why not? And off I went bombing around Dunedin for a while, waving at girls and looking cool. When I pulled back into the parking lot, I found this teenager, *a high school ballplayer,* with a crazed look on his face. Turns out, it was his car, and he thought I'd stolen it. He even called the cops and reported it missing. I calmed him down and things were fine, but Chacon and the other guys busted a gut. These veteran guys were not to be trusted.

I opened the season with Buffalo on the road against the Yankees' affiliate in Richmond, Virginia, not far from my home in Baltimore. My Mom and Dad and my Uncles George and Bill, the dieners, came along to watch my opening night as a pro. It wasn't too bad. I went 3-for-5 with a home run but got picked off first base with the hidden ball trick after my first base hit. Actually, a good thing because once you experience that level of embarrassment, it's likely never going to happen again. And it didn't. Plus my uncles got a memorable story. After the game, they went to a bar in Richmond and asked the bartender if they had any American beer, which happened to be the name of a popular but local Baltimore brand. "Sure," the bartender said, "We have all kinds of American beer—Budweiser, Miller—all kinds."

Thinking this pro game is not so hard after all, I faced Mel Stottlemyre in game two. Mel would go on to win 164 career games with the Yankees and join them in New York before the year was up and where we'd spend some time together in the early 1970s. Between his hard slider and disappearing sinker, I saw every pitch and thought I could hit them all. Net result, four strikeouts and a whole new outlook on this pro game thing. Had I been able to zoom ahead six months, I would see Mel starting three games in the World Series, and I probably wouldn't have felt so bad.

After about a week and a half on the road, the veterans invited me to one of their rooms for a postgame party. The rest is a blur, at least up to the point when I was experiencing the mother of all hangovers. As an initiation, those wankers pumped me full of cheap Carstairs whiskey and dumped me in my room. I woke up the next day and realized I had wet the bed, pooped myself, threw up, and looked like I'd been bleeding through my eyes. I was a freakin' mess. I felt like I needed to die to get better. Those guys had fun with me, and they weren't through. Somebody decided that I needed to learn how to chew tobacco. Well, I never had any affinity for tobacco, but I put just a little bit in my mouth and started chewing, trying hard not to swallow. Well, I got so sick, I don't know what kept me from puking. But somewhere in my tobacco delirium, our manager, Whitey Kurowski, the old Cardinal third baseman, sent me up to pinch hit. I'm seeing double at this point, and I remember thinking I'm seeing a couple of baseballs coming at me, thank goodness I'm holding a couple of bats. I got jammed, but managed to hit the ball off the very short right field fence in Buffalo's old War

Memorial Stadium, the same field they used in the movie *The Natural*. Feeling pretty unnatural, I was eyeballing my shot and tripped over first base, doing a nosedive into the dirt and scrambling on all fours back to first base, still feeling like death warmed over. Thank God there was no *SportsCenter* in those days, or they'd still be showing the clip. Everybody on the bench was mighty entertained.

The following spring I was once again back in the Mets' major league camp. You might have thought that I would have wised up, but I was still pretty clueless. I was listening to a couple of veteran guys talking. The topic was whether one man could lift three guys from the floor at one time. The smart thing for me to have done would have been to mind my own business and go run some laps or something, but instead I stuck my nose into the debate. "If the three guys were all as big as me, there was no way one guy could lift us all at once," I said, more than a few times, each time a little more vehemently than before. "All right, kid," the vets said, "Let's see. Here, you lie in the middle." Still in my uniform, I lined up between two of my beefier teammates. After I wrapped an arm around each guy's neck, they secured my legs so that we were one solid mass. The lifter was going to be the veteran outfielder Dick Smith and he would use both hands on my thick leather belt.

"Here, let me get a better grip," Dick said, taking hold of my belt. All at once, he pulled off the belt and undid my pants, while the men at my sides pressed in hard. Smith then pulled down the front of my shorts and unloaded a bottle of aftershave lotion, spraying a can of shaving cream onto my crotch. Rookies in the past had the shaving cream followed by a safety razor that removed a good bit of their pubic hair. I got off lucky and with no complaints; after all, I had practically begged them to do this to me.

Knowledge is not wisdom. Knowledge, someone said to me, was knowing that a tomato was a fruit. Wisdom was knowing that you don't put it in a fruit salad. I might not have been any wiser in that camp, but one thing had changed: I was now a married man. It was a somewhat unexpected development. Cecilia and I had planned to tie the knot in the fall, after the end of the baseball season. But as things developed, the Mets were not the only organization that had designs on employing a strong, young Maryland boy. So did the United States Army. And I did not want to go.

Not that I had anything against the army. I'm as patriotic as the next man. But my patriotism was colored by the sense of whether or not what my country was up to was right. I knew I didn't want any part of the war in Vietnam. The reasons are many, but not least of which is the fundamental belief that this war business is deadly, expensive, and not to be trusted. I had heard the powerful and ultimately convincing arguments that the Gulf of Tonkin incident was manufactured, and that the Domino Theory was bogus. No one was ever going to convince me that North Vietnam could be an existential threat to the United States.

I wasn't the only guy who felt this way, and in the early and middle 1960s, before the war heated up, deferments were abundant. I've read that as many as 60 percent of draft-age males in my time employed deferments to avoid active duty. You could, like Muhammad Ali, declare yourself a conscientious objector, which I was not. You could run to Canada, which I would not; I wasn't going to renounce my citizenship. You could join a National Guard or Reserve unit, like George W. Bush and a bunch of my Mets teammates did, or get a medical deferment for bone spurs, like Donald Trump, or go to Paris on behalf of the Mormon Church, and counsel the French on avoiding extramarital sex and alcohol, as Mitt Romney managed to do. Or like Dick Cheney, you could say "I have other things to do," and wangle a student deferment. I suppose I could have stayed at Maryland and done that.

There was another option, a deferment that was available only during the early years of the war. If you were married in 1965, you were clear of the draft. I was engaged to Cecilia. Our wedding was scheduled for the end of that season, which would become my rookie year with the Mets. Were I not a ballplayer, were I not in love, were I not seriously in question about the politics of this war, I wouldn't be chasing a deferment. But I was all of those things and the answer was Cecilia Hanna. We decided to get hitched early.

With our parents all on board, we drove to the justice of the peace in Chestertown, Maryland. In a quaint civil ceremony in a musty old building, with my Mom serving as witness and a 25-cent plastic, gold-colored ring from Woolworth's as a symbol of our commitment, Cecilia and I got semi-married. I say semi because we agreed not to consummate the marriage. Before we left, the justice of the peace's secretary gave us the customary gift bag including a box of detergent and a jar of Vaseline. Don't use it all in the same place, I'm thinking. Sly grins all around. Mom brought it back to reality, telling us, "You are married, but you are not married. Got it?" We came close to pulling that off, which is all I'm willing to admit. We were married in the Catholic Church the following October. Now fifty-four years later, we are still together and in love.

We had acted just in time. On the Monday following Chestertown, the selective service ordered me to report for my preinduction physical. Marriage certificate in hand, we quashed that, and headed off to Florida.

We spent our first month together in the Flamingo Motel in St. Petersburg, Florida, which was called "The City of the Newly Weds and Nearly Dead" back then, the latter for its appeal to retirees. The motel had a fabulous ornithological neon sign in front of a building badly in need of a paint job. It was headquarters for the Mets' winter instructional league. All of the players and coaches were there, all of them aware that the lights in our room went out early, but the newlyweds were not asleep.

The married-to-an-athlete thing had to be a shock to Cecilia. On her way to the motel laundry room, she was corralled by Clyde Mc-Cullough, one of our coaches, an old man in an aging stud's body. He regaled her for a half an hour on how to wash my shorts so I would avoid jock itch. Jock itch? Cecilia would learn all about that and those bloody strawberries on my ass and knees from sliding into bases.

With crazy young athletes in crappy motels, I wondered, did Cecilia need all this in her life? I doubt it. Baseball would come first in our relationship and, poor girl, she never wavered.

At the end of my rookie year, the marriage deferment was rescinded. Now I had to be a parent to avoid being drafted. I got another notice to report for a physical immediately. We didn't know it, but the solution was already in the works: once again, Cecilia came through. Back then they used what was called the "rabbit test." A woman's urine was injected into a female rabbit, and if the rabbit's ovaries swelled up, the woman was pregnant. Fatal surgery was required to examine the ovaries. Bad news for the rabbit, good news for us. Less than a week after the rabbit died and Cecilia's pregnancy was confirmed, we presented the results to the selective service. We were done with the draft.

Making the Team

In the spring of 1965, I had not yet reached my twenty-first birthday. I had produced one solid but unspectacular season in the minors, and during those sunny weeks in Florida, I produced a solid but unspectacular camp. I wasn't yet a consistent hitter; I certainly wasn't a consistent fielder. There was nothing in my performance that argued against me spending the summer of 1965 playing in Buffalo or some other minor league town. Except I had a peculiarity in the rules on my side.

In those years before the Major League Baseball draft, there was something called the first year rule. It was designed by the MLB owners to keep the wealthy teams from buying all of the amateur free agent talent with bonus money. The rule held that everyone who played one year of organized professional baseball was available to be drafted by another professional team. A team could protect its first year prospects in two ways. They could designate one first year pro who could be sent to the minor leagues, or they could put those players on their major league roster.

The Mets had already screwed themselves big-time, when they left Paul Blair unprotected. Blair was a great center field prospect who would end up winning four World Series rings. The Baltimore Orioles had snatched him up in 1964, and he promptly went on to lead the Eastern League in hitting at Elmira. Before I knew anything about the first year rule, the Mets had decided to avoid repeating this blunder, and resolved to protect four of us young first year guys on the big league roster: me, Tug McGraw, a right-handed pitcher named Jim Bethke, and an outfielder out of Rider College named Danny Napoleon. We spent the spring, in the words of Prince, doing something close to nothing, and then lo and behold, we all found out we would be going to war with Casey Stengel in Flushing, Queens, as members of the New York Mets, a terrible team entering its fourth year of existence.

Casey Stengel

Approaching my seventy-fifth birthday it's hard to believe that I'm about the same age as Casey Stengel was when he was managing the Mets in 1965. At training camp, he looked like an old man: gnarly body, bumpy and bent over a bit, hobbled by a leg injury with a taxi that left him with a big lump on his shin. All this at an age where losing height is easier than losing weight. I know because I'm there now. The Yankees had fired Casey after the 1960 season, considering him over-the-hill after he'd won them ten American League pennants and seven World Series. "I'll never make the mistake of being seventy again," Casey sarcastically said. The New York Metropolitan Baseball Club offered him the job of manager; Stengel jumped at the opportunity and ran with it. At my age, I can't imagine taking on the responsibilities of a big league manager; the only things moving fast in my world are time, technology, and young people texting. I struggle to remain relevant as I grow older when it seems most of what people want from me is the past. A past that I hope is prologue.

Too old for the Yankees was perfect for the Mets. The hire was genius. Casey knew that the essence of his job was entertaining "my writers," as he called them. He daily supplied the New York press with material, keeping them from going negative on the team, usually in his distinctive patois. "Been in this game a hundred years, but I see new ways to lose 'em I never knew existed," he said about the lovable 1962 team that lost 120 games. "Can't anybody here play this game?"

There were no yes or no answers in Stengelese. If Casey disliked the question or didn't want to answer it, "The Old Perfesser" took writers on rambling roundabouts through baseball history. It was a riff and a ruse. You might not remember the question when you got back. If he noticed me listening in, what I heard buried in the body of his diversion was a parable, directly applicable to something he wanted me working on, like hitting the cutoff man or knowing the game situation when I got on base. "Amazing strength, amazing power," he once said about me in a way that made me listen. "He can grind the dust out of a bat. He will be great—super—even wonderful. Now, if he can only learn to catch a fly ball." He was cagey and canny in a way I could never be. Few get to live concurrent

with their own legend. Stengel did, with an ancient face and dancing blue eyes when he smiled, which was often. I was fascinated then
and still am.

On a St. Patrick's Day, a writer asked, "Where's your green,
Casey?" "My players are green," Casey tossed off, "like Saboda here."
Stengel told Ed Kranepool, then twenty years old, "If you keep working on the things you're not good at, in ten years you have a chance
of being a star." Greg Goossen, a catcher and first baseman who was
too into gin martinis and late night card games, asked, "What about
me, Casey?" "Goossen, in ten years you got a chance of being thirty."
He was right on. Near the end of Greg's career, he was with the Phillies in spring training, and I asked how things were going. Goose
said, "I think I'm in trouble here. The other night the manager
caught me coming in after curfew." I said, "Well, maybe it won't be
so bad." "It wasn't just being late," he said, "there were four guys
carrying me."

I've never been much of a fighter. The last time I threw a punch
in anger happened during the winter instructional league in St. Pete,
and it involved Goose. Cecilia left to visit friends in Ocala. Me and
the boys went out for beers. When we got up to leave there was nothing but empty bottles on the table, and I swept a bunch of them
onto the floor. It was the stupid way to attract attention in a cracker
joint. We were followed out and everyone squared off for the show-
down. Goose jawed with a guy who suddenly whacked him in the
mouth. I launched a right at that guy—I still don't know if I hit
him—and it was on. Somebody jumped on my back, riding me to
the ground. I'm thinking this is where I get my ass kicked. Things
suddenly stopped. All they wanted was us out of there. We all piled
into my Pontiac Grand Prix. Goose, riding shotgun, held a hand-
kerchief on his lip, which needed stitches. A pitcher named Jay
Carden quietly puked in my backseat. I cleaned up the mess as best

I could. The lingering odor forced me to fess up to Cecilia that while she was gone I had strayed from the reservation.

Goose was a likable enigma. He had ability, but the gin derailed him. He became an actor, which few of his former teammates knew anything about. Gene Hackman handpicked him as his stand-in, which evolved into rough character roles in pictures like *Get Shorty, Waterworld, Wyatt Earp, Midnight in the Garden of Good and Evil,* and *Mr. Baseball*. Greg was sixty-five when he passed away in 2011 after a too-short intriguing life.

Growing Pains

I knew that Casey could spell my name correctly. He wrote it on his lineup card more than a few times in 1965. I would deliver 15 home runs for Casey—more than I ever hit in a whole season for anyone else—before he broke his hip and retired just after the All-Star break. He put me out there, even though I tried his patience.

One time, in old Busch Stadium, two stadiums back from where the Cardinals play today, I pushed him over the edge. It had been raining. The elderly grounds crew dragged the heavy tarp on and off two or three times. In the bottom of the ninth, we had a tenuous three-run lead. Tenuous because we were the Mets and the Cardinals loaded the bases with two outs. Dal Maxvill, who hit all of .135 that year, was up. The sun broke through over the third base dugout. It had been cloudy all day. I wasn't wearing my flip-down sunglasses. What were the chances I'd need them for one hitter?

Maxvill lofted a blooper over second base. I charged in and lost it in the newly discovered sun. It scooted by, three runs scored, and it was all on me. I was livid and embarrassed. When I got a chance to make amends in the top of the 10th, I popped up to right center. Heading onto the field after we were retired, I saw my helmet lying empty end up, and I was going to do it some damage. I stomped the helmet. It split open. My foot got stuck inside. I went into an emergency boogaloo trying to shake it off.

Casey bounded up the dugout steps like he's thirty again, pissed, a plaster cast on a right wrist he fractured a couple weeks earlier after an exhibition game in West Point against the Cadets. He grabbed my shirt with his left hand. I'm thinking, *He's going to crack me on the head with the cast and I'm standing in my helmet.* Stengel said, "Goddammit, Saboda, when you missed that fly ball, I didn't go in the clubhouse and throw your wristwatch on the floor. So, I don't want you busting up this team's equipment because you popped out. You're out of the game. Go sit down."

Well, shit. I was thinking I just fucked up my whole career. I went into the clubhouse through a door in the middle of the dugout, sat down alone, and couldn't stop the tears. Tom Hanks, managing the Rockford Peaches in *A League of Their Own,* tells his right fielder who's screwed up, "There's no crying in baseball." Well, yes there is. Especially when I had thoroughly fucked up a major league game and, I thought, my career with it. But after sitting me for a couple games, Casey put me back in the lineup. He never brought up the incident again—and I never forgot it.

The spring of 1964, when I was still with the big club, the Mets took an East Coast trip out of St. Pete to West Palm Beach, if that's not confusing. Mrs. Payson, the team's owner, threw the team a steak dinner. The wine pairing was Lancers Rosé. We got into it pretty good.

Casey took the microphone and regaled us with stories and advice. He knew money. He was a partner in a California bank. He counseled us about buying annuities and not spending all of our salaries, because for most of us baseball would end sooner than we thought. I paid attention. Cecilia and I lived within our means. He offered, "When you go out after a game, go with one or two guys, because if you go with four or five guys, by the time you buy back, you're drunk." There was laughter.

"I seen you out with ten guys," came the unmistakable New York accent of Duke Carmel, a journeyman having a solid spring. The discomfort settled into our testicles. Paul Simon, from Queens, called it "The Sounds of Silence." Stengel glared. "I've seen you out, too, Mr. Carmel, when you didn't see me. And another thing, you haven't made this team yet." Nope, and he never did. Back in St. Pete, the clubby emptied Carmel's locker. The moral to the story: Don't ever show up the Old Man.

Joe Pignatano—Piggy, as everyone, including his wife, calls him—is the only coach still alive from the field staff of the '69 Mets, and a Brooklyn native. He was catching for the Giants when the Mets purchased him in 1962. As soon as he could, he showed up at the Polo Grounds, the Mets home before they built Shea Stadium in 1964, and donned his new uniform before everyone else arrived. He walked to the dugout and found Casey alone. The two talked for twenty minutes. Jack Lang, a writer for the *Long Island Press* and the *Daily News*, dropped in and asked Casey who was catching that night. "Ah, that Pignatany guy, if he ever gets here." Another time, Casey asked Piggy to go to the bullpen as acting pitching coach because Red Ruffing was away scouting a young arm. The phone rang in the seventh. Casey told Piggy to get Nelson up. "Nelson?" There was no Nelson on the roster. "Yeah, Nelson." "Yessir." Piggy took a ball out of the bag, put it on the pitching rubber, and said, "Nelson, get up." Bob Miller picked up the ball and started loosening up. Piggy asked Miller, "When did you change your name?" Bob replied, "I didn't. He did." Piggy's last at bat in the majors with the Mets ended in a triple play.

Joe Durso wrote the biography *Casey*. Stengel signed a copy to my Mom, "To Mrs. Swoboda" (you can see where he first left off the "w" and then wrote over it, and I think my Mom corrected his spelling), continuing with, "The Producer of the Coming Star 'Ron,' a Future Hall of Famer—Casey Stengel." That's the only time I recall him using my first name.

After Stengel retired, we saw him during spring training with his wife, Edna. Cecilia and I were sitting in a restaurant with our baby, Ron Jr., who was having a rough time with colic. Casey and Edna, dressed to the nines, saw us and came over. Edna scooped up RJ and held him high above her head. It was a lovely gesture by Edna, who never had any kids. All I could think was, *Don't spit up now.*

At Mets Old-Timers' Days, Casey moved slowly into his uniform in the clubhouse. For his introduction, he mustered energy and seemed years younger. I could see the change. He skipped and danced around in front of the crowd. Pride, I guess. In 1970, I asked how Edna was doing. He got the saddest, faraway look on his face. "She's lost her mind." Alzheimer's. Casey was gone late in 1975, Edna followed a few years later.

Casey watched us win the Series. He sat to the left of the dugout in the front row, having a ball, giving interviews before the game and taking it all in. He was so much of those early Mets teams. I still can't believe my good fortune in playing for him. There were other men who could have handled the Yankee teams he took to pennants and World Series. Mrs. Payson paid him well to join the Mets. That had to be part of it. Then again, what better way to avenge what the Yankees had pulled on him? Take a manager's job in New York and live well. I asked Casey, "Would you have had this much fun if you had gone on to become a dentist?" He'd studied dentistry in his off-seasons as a player when dentistry was closer to plumbing. "If I would have become a dentist, I would have been an orthodontist because parents will buy things for their kids that they won't buy for themselves." I thought then and still do that this was wisdom speaking, straight ahead, no Stengelese.

Learning the Game

The next time I heard Stengel yell "Saboda, get a bat!" the team we were playing was the Houston Astros, who had followed the Dodgers into Shea. Turk Farrell, a hard-throwing right-hander, was on the mound late, and the Mets were trailing 7–3 after the Astros had scored four times in the top of the 11th.

Farrell had started the game and was still on the hill. Casey sent me up to hit for Roy McMillan, whose sharp fielding compensated enough for his mediocre hitting to put him in the fifteenth of what would turn out to be a sixteen-season career. I jumped a first pitch fastball from Farrell and hit it so hard that it cleared the back wall of the visiting bullpen in left field. It might have been the longest home run I ever hit. Next up, Danny Napoleon would single in his first at bat in the big leagues, and then with the bases loaded, Cleon Jones would single to drive in two runs. Exciting, but it was just enough for us to lose 7–6.

Afterward, a fan came into the tunnel outside our clubhouse and offered me the baseball. I didn't intend to sound arrogant, but I quoted a line I'd read from Babe Ruth: "That can't be the ball because you couldn't have gotten back this fast." I didn't take the ball, which shows how far I was looking ahead. I wish I had it on the shelf behind me in my office in New Orleans as I write this, but no. I did run into a fellow at a baseball memorabilia show who had the program from that day with a perfectly kept scorecard that showed my first major league home run. I traded him a signed baseball for it, and it hangs on my office wall under the last family photograph of my Mom. A fella shouldn't be so nonchalant about his first bomb.

My folks lived in Baltimore County, about a five-hour ride from Shea Stadium. When they came up to visit we would all stay in the Travelers Motel, just opposite LaGuardia Airport. A bunch of other players stayed there. It was a pretty good deal, and when we went on the road, the Travelers would put our stuff in a spare room and not charge us. At one point in the summer, my Mom and Dad drove up with a bushel basket full of blue crabs, steamed in the spicy Maryland style. The Travelers let us spread them out on a large table covered in newspaper and we proceeded to bang and crack and pick those crabs to the amusement and distraction of the rest of the restaurant. Sweet.

Things were speeding up for me on the field. On April 18, in the second game of a doubleheader, I played right field as we beat Gaylord Perry and the Giants 7–1. I took him deep for my only hit. Not bad. Then we were off to Los Angeles, my first trip to California. Tommy Lasorda was coaching for the Dodgers and invited me and Tug McGraw on a walk around Paramount Studios where they were shooting scenes for *Bonanza,* one of my favorite TV shows. Tug and I met Michael Landon, who played Little Joe Cartwright in the series. He let us handle his Colt .45. My world was getting bigger, quickly. On April 22, Casey started me in right field, and I went 1-for-3 against Sandy Koufax—my single drove in the only run in a 2–1 loss.

Then it was off to San Francisco where we stayed at the Jack Tar Hotel, right across the street from a place called Tommy's Joynt, full of bric-a-brac and collectibles of all sorts hanging from the ceiling and walls where you could eat buffalo meat in a stew that tasted a lot like roast beef. Tug's Dad, whom we were supposed to call Mac, came to visit from Vallejo, not far from San Fran. We drove over, and I saw the house where Tug grew up, met a couple of his neighbors, and road a little Honda motorbike that belonged to one of Tug's buddies and knew immediately that I wanted one. I traveled with a single lens reflex 35mm camera and hopped on one of the San Francisco cable cars and rode around snapping photos of this most beautiful city, including Coit Tower and Alcatraz Island.

On the 23rd of April, I pinch hit for Tug in the ninth, produced another bomb off Gaylord Perry as we scored four times to tie the thing up at eight on our way to winning it 9–8 in the 11th. This was getting to be fun. On the 25th, while Juan Marichal was shutting us out 5–0, I touched him for a pinch-hit single. It was of no consequence to the game, but Casey must have started thinking that, maybe, I should be in the lineup more. But where could he put me? Why not center field, where I had never played much as an amateur or a pro? In the nightcap of the double dip, that's where Casey started me. I rewarded his brilliance with a 2-for-5 game with a two-run home run off Ron Herbel and a run-scoring double off Bob Bolin, both right-handers. We won 4–3.

Houston

Houston, in 1965, was a fast-growing city made possible by the invention of air-conditioning and the decision of President Lyndon Johnson to base the National Aeronautics and Space Administration there. To me, that was the coolest thing: they were going to explore outer space. In high school almost all of my elective reading was science fiction: Robert Heinlein, Arthur C. Clarke, Isaac Asimov, Ray Bradbury, and others. I can still remember where their books were located in the library that's still standing at Sparrows Point High School. I also grew up with an illustrated book by Willy Ley called *Rockets, Missiles, and Space Travel* that outlined the history of rocketry. The book accurately projected rocketry's development through to the multistage equipment that would put men in space and eventually build huge space stations in orbit around

earth. I ate all this up long before 1968, the year that Stanley Ku-
brick's film *2001: A Space Odyssey* brought Clarke's book to life. I'm
not *A Space Odyssey* nut, but the movie captured my imagination,
especially the way the monolith kept appearing at all those crucial
moments in human history. Suggesting, perhaps, that life could
exist on a plane of pure energy.

As a young New York Met, baseball was getting most of my energy, not to exclude these dreams of outer space. Then, I waltzed
into the inner space of the Astrodome in 1965 and had my mind
completely blown. Both the dome and I were rookies in '65, and I
was agog. Billed as the Eighth Wonder of the World, to my eyes, it
was that and much more. Houston was a city on the rise, rich with
oil and tech, eager to join the big time. They already had an American Football League franchise, and were desperate for baseball. But
there was one big problem: the infernal heat. The Houston Sports
Association, headed by Roy Hofheinz, a former judge, state rep, and
mayor, walked the idea of a Houston club in front of Major League
Baseball in 1960. In return, he was awarded a new franchise that
would join the newborn Mets in bringing the National League to
ten-team parity with the American League, which had expanded
the year before. The Astros were born as the Colt .45's, symbolized
by a smoking six-shooter, and the team played outdoors in old Colt
Stadium until Colt Patent Firearms successfully sued them for
copyright infringement for using their name. So, in 1965, the team
renamed themselves the Houston Astros and the air-conditioned
Astrodome was built as "The Biggest Room in the World."

To minimize the amount of superstructure above ground level,
the playing field in the dome was excavated a couple of stories
below street level, so you got the same sense as walking into the Ca-
thedral of Notre Dame in Paris, in that it seemed bigger inside than
outside. In the case of the Astrodome, it was literally true. It was
wondrous at first sight: big and beautiful with a huge scoreboard

featuring a two-gunned cowboy who fired his pistols with sound and fury when an Astro hit a home run. The board lit up with the tracks of his "bullets" splaying all over the place while a couple of longhorn steers roared away as well. Quite a show, if a bit more retro than astro.

Building the Astrodome no doubt involved solving all kinds of novel engineering and construction problems, and it made indoor baseball possible. Yet, from the first exhibition games played at the end of spring training in 1965 between the New York Yankees and the Houston Astros, it became, in some cases, painfully clear that playing the game of baseball—the reason the Astrodome was built in the first place—was the last thing they'd thought about, if at all.

While they were busy checking off the myriad engineering problems they faced in putting up the biggest room in the world and patting themselves on the back for figuring out how to grow grass indoors, nobody thought about what happens when a fly ball travels across a background combining clear Lucite panels and the steel structure between them. Quickly they would figure out that in daylight, a baseball passing in flight against such a background would be hard to follow. It was like the ball was passing in front of a bright light that was flashing on and off behind it; the human eye just couldn't make the adjustment. Oh my. Houston, we have a problem. Popups and fly balls were dropping all over the place during the practices for that first exhibition game. Panic was in the air. They tried different colored balls . . . bright orange and such. Nothing helped.

What they had to do, they realized, was put some painters up on the Astrodome roof and coat their beautiful Lucite panels. It wasn't Picasso up there. After a couple of tries the pattern they settled on was a completely opaque pie-shaped segment that was roughly behind home plate. The rest was a thinner coating of paint that still managed to block the bright glare of the sun and made fly balls more visible again, which everyone agreed was a good thing. Except for the grass playing surface, which started thinning like an old man's hair before going completely bald. Unfortunately, their solution set the stage for a whole new bunch of problems.

In the outfield, even with the sun largely blocked, tracking fly balls against the interior roof structure was doable but hard. It put a lot more meaning into pregame practice, where you quickly figured out that you had better not ever take your eyes off anything up in the air, but even that didn't always work. One of the things you worked hard at as a pro outfielder was learning how to get an initial read on a fly ball and then, if necessary, turn away to run better and check out where the fence was. In the Astrodome, you wouldn't dare do this because when you took your eye off the ball during the pregame warmups, you discovered that too many fly balls would come down where you weren't. Not good.

The incredible disappearing grass got them through year one. But the ever-thinning surface made it clear that they needed some new thoughts on a playing surface. The dome authority turned to the Monsanto Corporation, who combined some ideas they had about indoor/outdoor carpeting and came up with what became known as AstroTurf. The Houston Oilers football team also had a home in the Dome, so you needed a surface that you could play baseball on and then roll up that carpet and lay down the football field.

They developed a short pile carpet that was laid over the dirt below with what felt like very little padding underneath. The rug debuted in the Astrodome in 1966 and what it did to the game of baseball wasn't pretty. Normal ground balls shot through the infield, creating baseball's first ever "AstroTurf hits," and changing the entire rhythm of the game. The turf also exacerbated second hop spin, which was always a part of the game but which became super-spin hops because of the short nap. That exploding second hop spin could really eat your lunch on the infield. In the outfield there was another concern. The turf produced these big Super Ball bounces that could hop clear over your head if you overcharged them; poorly struck bloop hits were suddenly kangarooing over the heads of outfielders and rolling to the wall for triples and inside-the-park home runs. No outfielder wanted that to happen, so fielders quickly concluded that the smart play was to back off, let the ball fall, and limit the damage to a single. It didn't always work; while you stood there waiting for the hop to drop, speedy runners would leg out doubles. Pretty goofy. "Will the skylight bother your team?" a reporter asked Stengel. "No," said Ol' Case, "we're still workin' on ground balls." A funny rejoinder, if only he had been kidding.

Nobody had invented turf shoes just yet, so we went into the Astrodome with our regular spikes and after a three-game series the bones in our feet hurt like hell. What was happening was that our cleats didn't dig into the turf. And with little padding we were literally standing on our cleats front and back with no support in the middle for our arches. The solution was to bring our old cleats. We always kept an old pair of "mudders," which we used when the field was wet so as not to mess up our better shoes. In those days the cutting edge in technology was leather soles with the steel cleats built into them while the uppers were made of kangaroo hide, which was thin and light. But if you got them wet, the kangaroo would stretch and your new shoes would get old very fast. Our contract with Rawlings only provided two pairs of shoes per season—hence, our mudders. On those, the cleats were worn down and worked just fine on the short nap of the AstroTurf.

Rusty Staub was a young outfielder with the Astros and his footwear solution was a bit more complex. Playing on the brand-new AstroTurf was causing him big hamstring problems, so Rusty would wear short soccer cleats in the outfield and on the bases. While at the plate he wore a regular steel-cleated baseball shoe on his left foot and changed once he got on base. While we stood around and waited.

Visiting Houston was always an adventure, but at one point in 1965 it became even more fun. We were invited to NASA headquarters to meet the Mercury astronauts Alan Shepard, Gene Cernan, John Glenn, and all those early guys. My outer-space wonder spilled over into one question after another. I kept my hand up and asked so many questions they had to quiet me down, but I was thrilled. These guys were all combat pilots and 100 percent heroes in my eyes. They still are.

School of Hard Knocks

Casey had made up his mind: I'd done enough to see a little more action. So, I'm starting now in center field in the Houston Astrodome where I take an 0-for-3 one night and then go 2-for-5, including an RBI double in a 12–9 loss. Here I am, the rookie starting center field for the New York Mets in my second professional season, with a base of baseball knowledge like an upside-down pyramid. I am so far ahead of myself, I might as well be in outer space. But here we go.

We finished my first ever major league road trip in Cincinnati playing at old Crosley Field, built for the Reds in 1912. For the first twenty-one years they called it Redland Field. It was the first ballpark equipped with lights and on May 24, 1935, the Reds beat the Phillies 2–1 in the first night game in the big leagues. All the runs were scored on fielder's choices. On April 30, 1965, we beat that for strange.

In the first inning, the Reds' righty John Tsitouris issued an intentional walk to lefty Ed Kranepool to load the bases with one out, setting up a double play situation with me coming up. I skied a fastball to center field. In Cincinnati, the center field wall was only 380 feet away from home plate. The first ten feet was cinder block, topped with a yellow line above which was a home run. Beyond that line, and set back about four inches from the concrete wall, was a plywood wall, painted dark green, installed to prevent the batters from looking into the headlights of the cars on the nearby elevated highway. My fly ball banged straight to the ground off the wooden barrier and should have been ruled a grand slam home run.

Vada Pinson, in center, seemed to concede it with an underhand toss back toward the infield. But Frank Secory, the second base umpire, ran out ruling the ball in play. Joe Christopher, our runner at second base, was tagged up and only made it to third. I crushed the ball about as hard as I ever could, and all I got for my efforts was a single and an RBI. Art Shamsky, who platooned in right field with me on the 1969 Mets, was on the Reds then and told me he thought it was a home run. I was credited with two grand slams in my career; that's one that got away.

Making matters worse, Jim Hickman was up next, and he grounded into a double play. My out-of-the-park single produced the only run we scored on Tsitouris, who went all the way for a 6–1 win. Best thing I got from it was a great Yogi Berra story. Yogi, our first base coach, charged out there arguing like hell and got thumbed out by John Kibler. After the game, in the closeness of the tiny visitors' clubhouse, the writers all went right to Yogi's locker to find out what he said to get the heave-ho. As only Yogi could, he said, "All I told 'em was, if you couldn't hear that ball hit the wood, you're blind." We all nodded, knowing exactly what Yogi meant.

The next day, Saturday, May 1, was a CBS *Game of the Week*, and I was back in the lineup in center field. Another unique and troublesome thing about Crosley Field was that, instead of a warning track, it had an incline running up to the wall that started more steeply in left field and tapered down as you moved toward right. So, in center, you were advised to play a couple of steps up on the hill so it didn't surprise you going back on a ball. In the seventh inning, while we were on our way to getting our asses handed to us 9–2, Frank Robinson was facing Larry Bearnarth with runners at first and third. Frank hit a bullet toward me in center. Perched up on the ramp, I immediately made the wrong read and headed down to flat ground, before almost immediately realizing that the hill was a lot higher than I had thought. So, I started to back up the slope, but before long I fell flat on my butt, looking up just in time to see Robinson's liner whiz past me. It banged into the cinder block wall and caromed by me about two feet on my left, heading smartly back in the direction from whence it came. Fortunately, while I was doing my impression of a turtle on his back, our shortstop Roy McMillan had retrieved the ball in short center and somehow held Robinson to a single and one RBI. He might have been laughing so hard he forgot to run. Some of my embarrassment was relieved when I took Sammy Ellis deep for one of our runs, but not much. "I've been around 100 years," Casey said later, "and he makes plays you ain't never seen before."

I always knew that the primary reason I was a major leaguer was that I could hit with power, but I had had the sense as I was coming up that I wasn't anything but a capable fielder. Upon arriving at Shea, more than a few outfielders had trouble adjusting to the stadium's high triple-decked seating. The background was inconsistent, and chimerical atmospherics played with the lighting, especially during day games when the sun was in and out or it got misty. It was a challenge to pick up the ball off the bat. You wanted to be on edge, but under control. Instead, I was always anxious. I made every mistake doubt could spawn. This happens when you're in the big leagues too soon and don't know how to play baseball.

I was a mess. One day I was in right field and there was a popup behind second, clearly belonging to the second baseman, Billy Gardner. I nuzzled in behind him, hoping to schmooze the play along. He was all ready to catch it when I suddenly yelled, "Take it!" Hearing that, Billy jumped out of the way, allowing the ball to fall for a hit. I was left standing there thinking, *What the fuck just happened?* I hadn't been told the simple rule that if you want it as an outfielder, you sing out; otherwise, you keep your mouth shut. It can't be a conversation. Too late to make me feel better, I saw that same play by a veteran, Matt Holiday, playing left field for the Cardinals in a World Series game. You could read, "Take it" on his lips as the shortstop let the ball fall. Yowie.

Later, the Mets used me in left field, with Bud Harrelson at shortstop. He'd cover as much of left field as I would let him. That was the rub. On in-between fly balls I'd break in, not always sure about the play with Buddy charging my way. He wouldn't break off, and here I'd come like the thundering buffalo, calling for the ball late or not at all, and running straight through Buddy's 145 pounds. It wasn't pretty.

After two more losses to the Reds we returned to Shea to meet the Phillies, and I was still the starting center fielder. In the second game, Jim Bunning shut us out on a four-hitter, supplying himself the only run he needed with a home run off Warren Spahn in the sixth inning. I got one of our four hits but managed to taint it. I ripped a Bunning fastball into the left field corner, but I tripped over first base as I was eyeballing my drive and turned what should have been an extra base hit into a single. You have to look out for those little white things out there in the dirt.

The Milwaukee Braves cruised into Shea with Henry Aaron and company. I hit a two-run home run off Tony Cloninger and a solo shot off Phil Niekro, and we won it 4–2; I also kicked a ball in center. People were getting used to young Swoboda, who giveth and who taketh away, but I was still in center field when the Cardinals came to town. There was big talk about my first matchup with Bob Gibson. It couldn't have been worse: Gibby shoved it up my pooper with four strikeouts and hardly a loud foul. We lost 4–3.

Sandy Koufax

After overdosing on Bob Gibson, it was almost a relief to face Sandy Koufax. Almost.

When I batted against Sandy Koufax in his final two seasons, I was too focused on my at bats to think much about what a beautiful pitcher he was. Only later, after he retired, did I appreciate his balletic grace and elegance on the mound. Hollywood handsome, he had a lean, angular body, and long fingers that Vladimir Horowitz could only envy. His four-seam fastball jumped at you. His true 12-to-6 curveball with great rotation was always a curveball even when it arrived high in the strike zone. I don't remember Koufax trying to crowd me inside or going away. His detachment through the whole process said, *Here it is, right where you want it. If you can hit it, fine. If you can't, that's okay, too.*

I can't imagine that Sandy saw me as a particular threat. The fastball was coming whether you were Ron Swoboda or Hank Aaron. I handled the heater pretty well back then. I can remember a couple of at bats when I squared up Koufax fastballs pretty good. The first time I sent a rocket on two nasty hops that ate up third baseman Junior Gilliam. The ball seemed to hit both ankles as it went through his legs and down the left field line for a double. The second one was a bomb that I jerked into the left field stands off a 3–2 heater. In his twelve-year career, Koufax gave up 204 regular season homers to a total of 110 hitters, and I'm one of them. When you go long ball on a pitcher, they remember you, and Koufax remembers me.

Sandy attended the University of Cincinnati for baseball. He walked on the Bearcat freshman basketball team. He's remained a college basketball fan. During the 2003 NCAA Basketball Final Four, we both happened to be in the New Orleans Superdome. I saw Sandy sitting courtside and went down to say hello. He was polite but busy, and I kept the conversation short. On the way back to my seat I passed two New Orleans Zephyrs, David Matranga, a middle infielder, and a pitcher, Brandon Puffer. They'd seen me yapping with Koufax and were impressed that I actually knew him. For laughs, I kicked it up a notch.

"How many people do you think are in the Dome right now?" I asked.

They guessed in the middle fifty-thousands.

"You know how lucky that makes you?"

"Lucky? Why?"

"There's 55,000 people in the Superdome, and the only SOB here to ever take Sandy Koufax deep is standing right in front of you." I got the laugh I was after.

On the mound or off, no one resembled him. Sandy Koufax was already the legend when I first faced him. Bob Gibson could be viscerally intimidating, full of in-your-face anger. Personal rage, fastballs too close to your noggin. He didn't mind if he hurt anyone. He liked it. Long into his playing days, I rolled a seeing-eye single through the infield and that was the first hit I ever got off him. I'm as proud of that cheesy single as I am of my two two-run homers that beat Steve Carlton 4–3 the evening he threw "the best stuff I ever had" for 19 strikeouts. Koufax seemed detached, the businessman whose job was delivering marvelous pitches to John Roseboro, his catcher and muscle around the plate. At a play at home, I came in standing up. Roseboro tried to jam a hard tag on my cup. My right thigh, striding forward, blocked it. As a hitter, I felt incidental in Koufax's entire process. Sandy was above it all.

Daily Life

I am a pretty sociable guy, and I've never had much trouble making friends. Right from the start on the Mets, I made friends with
two guys: Ed Kranepool and Tug McGraw, who remained pals
with me for as long as we possibly could.

Ed was a big first baseman who was the first young player signed
to the Mets. Born to a Jewish family in the Bronx, a graduate of James
Monroe High School, Ed was an all–New York guy who was blessed
to have been able to spend his entire career with a New York team.
He was part of the legendarily awful 1962 expansion Mets, and part
of the legendary Miracle Mets of 1969. Fans identified with him.

Tug was an exuberant Californian, always ready with a joke. In
New York that rookie year, we both stayed in the Travelers Motel.
We made friends with one of the special cops who worked the home
dugout at Shea. Freddy Amarada lived with his large Italian family
in Brooklyn. Tug and I would go there for Sunday dinners, eating
incredible amounts of Italian food washed down with good Italian
red. Too much food. Even now, when I hear the word "mangia" I
get uncomfortable. Occasionally, Tug and I would hop the number
7 train outside Shea and head into Manhattan, no forethought, no
connections, just two tourists on missions of discovery. One time,
Tug talked our way into the audience for the taping of the Johnny
Carson show. Mostly, we were simply two waifs wandering around
in a city bigger than my dreams, dwarfed by buildings, our eyes big,
like the ones Margaret Keane finally got credit for painting.

On the road, Tug roomed with Ed Kranepool, but we all hung
out together, occasionally, drinking mai tais in the room on an
afternoon of an off-day on the road. Every day on the road we would
order room service. Every day we would look at the fancy menus,
the lobster and the steak, and every day we would order cheeseburg-

ers. Every day. Medium rare, if you please. With French fries. You get no points for leading the league in cheeseburgers. Afterward, a three-man wrestling match might break out. One time in Philadelphia, we put together water balloons and tossed them out the window onto an unsuspecting world below. Being in the major leagues meant getting paid to play a kids game. I think a part of us never did want to grow up.

Kranepool and I were buddies, too. We made friends with Vinny Bennich, the manager of the Gaslight Café, which in the early 1960s was a place where you could see Bob Dylan and other folk acts, but was now a Playboy Club–like operation. One night, Krane and I went into the city to buy some clothes. Eddie knew a guy who sold Pierre Cardin suits at cost and we both picked up a couple each. The plan was to pick up the suits and join Vinny Bennich for dinner and drinks at the Gaslight. We didn't want to leave the suits in boxes in the car so we locked them in the trunk for safekeeping. The night went long; we left the Gaslight after midnight and found the lot where we had paid to leave the car with the suits in the trunk. Right? Wrong. The lot was closed, the car was stolen, and our never worn suits were never seen again.

Eddie and I shared another friend, a wonderful guy, a comedian and actor named Jackie Wakefield who passed away back in 2010. We became acquainted with Jackie after he performed as the after-dinner entertainment at one of the New York Mets welcome home dinners, held every year before the team opened the regular season, one year after Richard Pryor. Jackie was probably considered a second-line comedian who worked the Borscht Belt, the series of resorts in the Catskill Mountains, but he was a first-rate guy. Besides appearing in clubs, Jackie made a lot of commercials for brands, including Schaefer Beer, Gillette, United Airlines, Almond Joy, Alcoa, Yankee Franks, and Esso, which made him a big financial success. He lived with his wife and family in New Rochelle, New

York, where he kept a sixty-foot power boat moored off the East River. On one particular off-day, Jackie invited us out for a spin on the water.

The plan was to get an early start on a cruise around Manhattan, getting back to New Rochelle before dark, but the weather decided not to cooperate. When Krane and I met Jackie at his boat, the rain had begun falling on what promised to be a thoroughly miserable day. After a couple gin and tonics, Jackie had a brainstorm. "Since this boat isn't leaving the dock," he said, "let's drive into Manhattan and have a drink at Toots Shor's." Toots Shor's was a restaurant and lounge in Midtown on 51st Street. It was the place to be back then. Toots, a former bouncer with plenty of rough edges, was a big fan of almost anybody famous in sports and entertainment.

It was a great idea, given the weather, except for one problem. We were in our boating outfits, and in those days you didn't drop into Toots Shor's or any halfway decent joint in Manhattan wearing jeans, sneakers, and sweatshirts. "No problem," said Jackie, "I got a closet full of clothes and we look like about the same size. I can fix you up." So, we went to Jackie's house.

We got there and dove in. Silly as it sounds, we were having a ball playing dress-up with Jackie's clothes. Before we knew it, we were walking down 51st Street and into Shor's place. We sat in the lounge at a little cocktail table and a waiter came to take our order. I asked for a Dewar's Scotch and water. The way they served it was with the shot straight up, neat with water and ice in a separate glass, and they'd ask you if you want it mixed. "Sure," I said, and that's where the fun began. The waiter dumped the shot of Scotch into my glass, splashing some onto my pants. All over the comic moment, Jackie said, "Hey, watch what the hell you're doing," causing the waiter to snap back, "You act like they're your pants." As Krane and I start to giggle, it's like this was rehearsed. Wakefield, with perfect timing, comes back with, "As a matter of fact, they are my pants, and I'll tell you another thing," pointing at Kranepool, "watch out for that son of a bitch over there, because those are my pants, too." By now the three of us were on the floor, and the waiter's like, "What's so fucking funny?" A totally inside joke, a totally unique situation. We let the waiter in on it and we all had a laugh.

I was also close to Cleon Jones and Tommie Agee. They were good guys who told great stories, and since we were all outfielders, we spent a lot of time together in practice and got to know one another. Cleon, with his deep Southern accent, loved to tell yarns about the guy back home in Mobile who was such a good fisherman, he could turn on the faucet, and he would catch fish from it. When my Mom and Dad would visit from Baltimore, they'd bring a bushel of steamed blue crabs and Cleon and Tommy, along with pitcher Al Jackson, when he was with the club, would join us in tearing into them. Cleon and I are still close. A couple of years ago when we appeared together at a fantasy baseball camp, Cleon confessed that for years when we played together, he maintained a friendship with Louis Armstrong, occasionally stopping by the home Louis kept in Queens for barbeque after a doubleheader on Sunday. "Get out of here!" I shouted. Armstrong, from my time in New Orleans, was long one of my favorites, and a great baseball fan, who used to sponsor an amateur team in New Orleans. What I would've given for a conversation with Louis Armstrong. Wow!

Hard Ball

In late June, we took three out of four from the Reds to finish a 7–4 home stand. I had three hits in the game we lost and drove in a pair, with another home run in game four. Then we hit the road, and the road hit back. In Milwaukee, I touched up Cloninger for a three-run shot, but that was all we got, and he beat us 4–3. I drove in a run in each of the next three games, which, similarly, we lost. To run the downer to six losses in a row would require the worst day I ever had in the outfield, which I recounted earlier, a game that included failure, a tantrum, a reprimand from the manager, and tears. But it was all part of growing up, and Casey, thankfully, hadn't given up on me.

Off we went to Philadelphia, a town we hated. Where the hell did they come up with the "City of Brotherly Love"? That might be what William Penn had in mind when he named the place, but he never had to play baseball there. The fans were coarse and the ballpark was old Connie Mack Stadium, which looked like a factory from the outside. My Dad had come up from Baltimore with a couple of my uncles to watch the game and say hi to Gus Triandos, the Phils' catcher who had worked with my dad at Fox Chevrolet. Gus had been my boyhood idol, when he was hitting home runs for my hometown Orioles. Now he was in the final ebb of his career. As usual, he greeted my Dad by saying, "Hey, you old bald-headed SOB, how you doin'?" My Dad called Gus a "big, dumb Greek," and both of them laughed.

We took an opening doubleheader from the Phils, beating Bunning and Chris Short. I don't know how many times those two were swept in a twin bill, but it couldn't have been often. Casey kept me in right field in game three, which would lead to one of the oddest plays I ever made. In the midst of an ugly first inning during which we gave up a five-spot, Triandos, one of the slowest humans ever to play Major League Baseball, found himself on third base with one out. Cookie Rojas hit a line drive that I tracked down running away from home plate. Thinking that Gus would tag at third and score easily, I hustled the ball into Kranepool, the cutoff man. Almost an afterthought, Ed relayed the ball to the catcher, who slapped the tag on the lead-footed Triandos.

"Yer out!" thumbed the umpire. I had never seen someone thrown out tagging up from third on a relay play at home. Ever and I don't think I ever will.

July promised continued success. On July 5, with the dazzle of fireworks still in our eyes, I exploded against the Cubs in a double-header in Chicago. In game one, I knocked in all three of our runs with a three-run home run off Dick Ellsworth, and we won 3–2. Back in the lineup for game two, I went 2-for-2 with my 15th home run and my 36th and 37th RBIs of the season off Bill Faul. We then capped the sweep 3–0, behind Tom Parsons's complete game six-hit shutout. Solid stuff for the Mets and yours truly. I felt great. But as it turned out, those would be our last wins and my last home runs and RBIs of the first half. The club dropped its final three games before the break. My .249 average with 15 homers and 37 RBIs had me mentioned in Rookie of the Year talk, but in truth, it was like the joke about fifteen hundred lawyers at the bottom of the ocean . . . a nice start. "This is ridiculous," I said to one reporter. "Who am I to be hitting all these homers?" The pitchers around the league began asking themselves the same question, though not with the same starry-eyed sense of wonder. Had my rookie season been a stock, this would have been the moment to have shorted me.

I had driven home to Baltimore for the All-Star break. (the National League won 6–5, for the third straight year; the Mets' lone representative, my buddy Ed Kranepool, did not play). I worked out with my old amateur team, Leone's Boys Club. Walter Youse was still the manager. He was always known to be a bit of a racist who never had black kids on the team, and that was still the case. When I arrived, I immediately noticed this lean, well-muscled off-white-looking kid on the squad who could really hit. His name was Reginald Martinez Jackson—Reggie Jackson—before he would hit 563 home runs, which is now good for fourteenth on the all-time list and sixth when he retired. Before he would find superstardom on

George Steinbrenner's Yankees of the late 1970s, this "Spanish" kid, according to Walter Youse, was something. But nobody knew that then, least of all me. I was more concerned with what was hurting my swing, which I wasn't able to fix on a three-day break in Baltimore. All I knew was to keep hacking.

We picked up on our three-game losing streak with another seven losses in a row, in the midst of a spell when we would win a meager four of 29 games. But during that time, we suffered a more significant setback.

Casey Stengel, with his wrist still in that cast, closing in on his seventy-fifth birthday, had made all sorts of jokes to downplay the injury, talking about how he could use the heavy plaster cast on a pitcher who wasn't ready to be taken out of the game. He was in pretty good shape for someone his age, looking forward to the Old Timers' game at Shea on Saturday, July 24, at which time the Mets planned to celebrate Casey's big day, since his actual birthday was the 30th of July, and we'd be on the road.

The ceremony at Shea was for the public. The real birthday party would be after the Old Timers' Game, Saturday night at Toots Shor's. As a rookie, I wasn't invited to any of this, but according to Maury Allen's Stengel biography, *You Could Look It Up* (one of Casey's favorite lines), "The Party at Shors was splendid. The food was magnificent, the drinks were endless and the laughs were enormous." According to Allen, "Sometime late in the evening, Casey, weary and slightly inundated with booze, walked into the men's room. He slipped on a wet floor, felt some painful twisting in his side, struggled to his feet and said nothing about it."

With an undiagnosed broken hip, Casey kept pounding drinks, closed the joint, and went home with the Mets' comptroller, Joe De-Gregorio. Not until 8 a.m. the next morning, with the pain increasing, did Stengel ask DeGregorio to call the team's trainer, Gus Mauch, who in turn summoned the team physician, Peter LaMotte, who in turn scheduled surgery to implant a steel ball joint where Casey's hip had fractured.

As the team continued its nosedive with interim manager Wes Westrum, one of Casey's coaches, at the helm, Casey tried hard to act like a man on the mend. Through sheer willpower, Stengel had fought his way through countless injuries over the years, but at seventy-five he had to face the inevitable: his run of fifty-five years in uniform was over. "You can't go out to the mound hobbling and take your pitcher out with a cane," he explained. With a little pomp and a lot of ceremony, he retired, with the Hall of Fame announcing that the man who piloted seven World Championship teams would merit immediate induction. Casey headed home to Glendale, California, to complete his recuperation. The episode had generated a batch of fan mail for the ailing "Ole Perfesser," which the Mets eventually shipped to California. Casey's wife, Edna, answered one letter from a ten-year-old with the note: "Casey thinks the Mets will be in the World Series before you are in high school." Which was hysterically optimistic at the time and almost right on the money.

The taciturn Westrum got the interim removed from the manager's title and took over as Stengel's replacement. Westrum was highly regarded as a catcher and coach with the San Francisco Giants who "read" pitchers' motions to detect their pitches ahead of delivery. A valuable talent that had helped Willie Mays, who didn't need a whole lot of help, to a few more base hits and home runs. As a manager, Wes was often inscrutable and uninspiring. His best endorsement might have been that he came cheap.

Certainly he had no answers for me as my season did a U-turn. The NL had figured me out, and I would never, in my nine-year big league career, have the productive run I had in the first half of 1965. It does seem that in trying to handle so many sliders, the radius of my swing got too long and slowed my bat down. Playing under Casey was the strongest offensive run of my career—I hit four

homers and drove in 13 the rest of the way and never again matched
that level of power. The game would seem a lot harder, and I would
work at making myself a better outfielder. But the promise of those
early days when I made it impossible for Casey not to play me would
settle into something less. I'd manage nine years in the big leagues,
no disgrace, and I had quite a few memorable moments. On
July 4, 1966, I hit a ball onto the left field roof in Connie Mack
Stadium in Philadelphia, and a month later I smashed a three-run,
pinch-hit, walk-off home run to beat the Giants 8–6 at Shea. The
pitcher was poor Bill Henry, a solid pro with a respectable sixteen-
year career, who I banged around like a piñata. In April 1968, I
homered in four consecutive games, then added one a few days
later off Chris Short in Philadelphia to give us a 1–0 win, which was
good enough to earn me a spot on the cover of *Sports Illustrated*.
The cover line said "Slugger Ron Swoboda," and I must say I
looked pretty good.

But I never felt like I had any of it coming. There were times
when I was so hot that I seemed to justify the highest expectations people had of me. The pure high of those auspicious begin-
nings would never return, even though that early power and its
unpredictable reappearances earned me a lot of forgiveness, and
some popularity. But looking back on it from all these years down
the road, I still can't help but wonder what I lost when Casey left.

During the rest of the 1965 season, Westrum did nothing to
threaten the Mets' tradition of last place finishes, and management,
having invited Stengel back after every losing year, brought Westrum
back as well. The following season saw Wes earn the distinction of
being the first Mets manager to avoid losing a hundred games. To
complement the raw "Youth of America" that we youngsters rep-
resented, the front office collected a bunch of proud old pros who
were on their last legs. That combo managed to set a new standard
for the club, finishing up in ninth place with a 66–95 record. Close

observers saw progress; at the end of July, we were only eight games under .500, before the old arms and legs fell off in the dog days. While the team did better, I did worse. My average loitered at .222, and I hit only eight home runs. The whole experience left the front office more committed than ever to Casey's Youth of America; we were young, and we made mistakes, but management was willing to suffer through our learning process. I guess they felt they owed the same latitude to Wes, and brought him back for 1967. Me, they decided to send to Puerto Rico to play winter ball. They thought I'd profit from the playing time. Really?

Puerto Rican Baseball

"The definition of an adventure is something that really shouldn't happen to you." It's a quote from my friend, the Black Mountain poet and *Village Voice* columnist Joel Oppenheimer, who I drank with at the Lion's Head Tavern, him sipping measures of bourbon, me Dewar's on the rocks. Playing for the Criollos de Caguas (Caguas Creoles) in the 1966 Puerto Rican winter league, the team bus rides through the mountains were adventures, man. Scary. Over the highlands on narrow, winding roads, no shoulders or guardrails, hardly room for the bus, the driver fresh out of the Bob Bondurant School of race car driving. It was harrowing. Because baseball doesn't get easier after a near-death experience, I scrunched low in the seat, burying my head under my jacket or anything available, and under no circumstances looked out the window.

I don't know what I thought I knew about Puerto Rico. I wasn't sure if I needed some security in the house. I've always bought into the line from Arthur Jones, inventor of the Nautilus weight training machines, that you don't need a gun very often, but when you do, you need it real bad. On the plane down I had two pistols secured under the diapers and bottles in our son Ron Jr.'s baby bag: a .22 Colt Woodsman and a .38 Colt Single Action Army. As it turned out, I was being melodramatic. The only time I had to use them was New Year's Eve. I fired rounds into the air to celebrate. Nobody in the neighborhood noticed. They were busy blasting away themselves.

Cecilia, my son, and I lived in a house on Calle Diamante, the street of diamonds. Our transportation was a Honda 175 motorcycle that I'd crated up and shipped to the island. Cecilia and I rode all over the place on this small bike. We loaded up on the Honda with our kid squeezed between us. Our favorite run was into El Yunque, the rain forest—jungle the way it should be: overgrown, birds, and clamor. Nobody wore helmets, and I kept the .22 pistol stuck in my belt. I can only shake my head at our recklessness. I shiver at the age of almost seventy-five at all that could have gone wrong.

What did go wrong was the baseball. I had just finished a trying major league season with the Mets. Those readers who have never played the game might be surprised how the little nicks and bruises and muscle strains accumulate, and sap your strength. On little rest I'd headed straight into more baseball.

The Mets had made the deal because they thought more ball would speed my development. It was hard to tell at the time. This was quality competition, rosters thick with major league talent, including the finest native Puerto Rican players. I got off to a fast start, swinging the bat well, including a couple of home runs, and then went brain-dead. Burnout and massive homesickness set in. At Christmas I sprang for the airfare to import my folks, and Cecilia's Mom, Dad, and sister from Maryland. Fun, but it didn't fix things on the field.

Dad and my father-in-law, Bill Hanna, were walking around the neighborhood and met a woman of the night in broad daylight. They were dressed in clearly *turista* attire. She thought she'd found two live ones. I'm not sure they understood what she was trying to sell. For the first couple of blocks they thought she was trying to be friendly. Once they caught her drift, they didn't dicker and made a run for the house, where Cecilia and our gang had been watching the show through the picture window.

Even with my game in a crisis stage, before the novelty faded, there was enjoyment to be had. This was our first trip outside the continental U.S. The only familiar thing was the currency, American dollars. We adjusted easily. It was enlightening to meet Puerto Ricans who had not left the island, stable family people with an exuberant culture. Most of the Spanish I speak comes from evenings spent after games at a bar called the Chicken Inn. I went from being a baseball player in Queens to a *pelotero* on the island. That was exotic. I drank with the locals, who took to calling me Ron Con Soda, though my usual was a rum and cola with a lime twist, Cuba Libre. Alcohol isn't supposed to help the memory. But brands like Palo Viejo—Old Wood, *el barman, por favor!*—a respectable local rum, and Ronrico have never faded from my mind.

The brio Puerto Ricans brought to the ballpark was far better humored than what I was used to in unruly places like Wrigley Field, where the girl who looks fifteen yells "Fuck you, Ron!" Or as she pronounced it, "Ran." At Fenway *Pack* it sounded like, *Fack you, number farteen!* A hot day in Mayagüez, concession stands were selling thick-skinned oranges called *chinas*. The vendors turned them on a lathelike contraption, shaving the rind and punching holes in one end. The folks squeezed and sucked out the juice. What remained was a deflated missile. Sometime around the fifth inning, *fanáticos* in the upper section of the right field bleachers started jawing with the fans sitting on folding chairs in front of them. Next thing *chinas* were flying everywhere back and forth. A happy little riot without anger or punches. We enjoyed it from the dugout—the laughing and flying *chinas*—until the umpires delayed the game and ended our entertainment.

Joe Foy played third base for the Criollos. He was an amusing fellow a year older than me. Cecilia, the kid, and I liked to hit the beach with him and his wife, Sadie. He was a dark-complexioned black man who favored ebony bathing trunks for the double takes he drew. He was always upbeat in Puerto Rico, did comical shit. Nothing indicated the drug problems that ruined his career and his life. Some of us white guys put burnt cork under our eyes to deal with glare from the stadium lights. Foy disappeared into the clubhouse and returned with shaving cream under his eyes. He got his laugh. Today, Joe would have lit up Twitter.

Onward

On the face of it, you'd have to say the Puerto Rican experience paid off. During the 1967 National League season, I hit 13 home runs and a career-high .281. I guess management knew what it was doing, even though technically the average benefited from five bunt base hits. Ordinarily a team doesn't want its home run threat to go around bunting, but those five wimpy singles were worth about 12 total points on my average. On the other hand, maybe everybody should have bunted more, because we unfortunately demonstrated that the Mets had not lost the address of last place nor the knack for losing at a three-digit pace. Westrum was let go right before the season ended, right before we moved into three-figure territory in the L column.

I had the task of negotiating a new contract. I didn't have an agent. They were rare then, for superstars, maybe. One-on-one, I took my raw numbers into my meeting with Mets GM Johnny Murphy, an all-star reliever on the Ruth, Gehrig, DiMaggio Yankee teams. He'd taken me for a good dinner on a road trip, and that was my first taste of red wine, which he considered better for controlling weight than beer. We negotiated to his offer of $28,000, a surprisingly decent number, nearly doubling my salary. I suggested thirty grand as a nicer round number. That would allow Cecilia and me to move out of the cheesy apartments we'd been renting and to buy our first house. To my amazement, he nodded yes. Here's the catch. This was January. I wouldn't begin collecting the bucks until the regular season started in April. I sat in the Shea Stadium parking lot, my hands shaking on the steering wheel of my Grand Prix, worrying about all the time that had to pass and all that could occur before I would get my mitts on the money. I drove home at 25 miles per hour, scared shitless that something would happen to me before I could get paid.

Today, if you call up the Mets records between 1965 and 1968, the seasons all look kind of the same. We finished 10th, 9th, 10th, and 9th (or last, second to last, last, and second to last). Our records during the first three of those years were 50–112, a much better 66–95, and 61–101.

The outlier was 1968, Gil Hodges's first year, when we climbed to 73–89. The patience exhibited by the front office was at last being rewarded. By Labor Day that season, we had played well enough to be in contention for sixth place. That may not seem like much progress to fans accustomed to the pace of today's game. Today, during the Christmas holidays, a team can sign a couple of free agents and turn themselves into a contender; by the same token, if by the All-Star Game a team is underachieving, an astute GM can trade his talent to a contender in exchange for some up-and-comers. In the 1960s, teams built slowly, if for no other reason than that they could. Teams controlled players; free agency didn't exist. GMs were conservative about surrendering talent.

But our front office kept building from within. In 1967, Tom Seaver joined the team, went 16–13, closed out the National League's memorable 15-inning, 2–1 victory in the All-Star Game, and every fifth day gave his team confidence that we could win. We had all known how daunting it was to try to sleep the night before facing Gibson or Koufax or Marichal. Now we had a sleepless-night guy of our own. The following year, Jerry Koosman joined the team full-time and won 19 games. Now we had two, with more on the way. A year or two earlier, we were the Last Chance Saloon, the place where pitchers came when they wanted to see if they could eke out one final season in the show. Now we were the home of Young Studs.

One stat will tell you everything about the difference these guys were making. In 1965, the staff allowed 752 runs. In 1966, 761 runs. In 1967, 672 runs. In 1968? Opponents scored 499 runs, a 26 percent drop. Of course, we still only scored 473 runs.

We also had Gil Hodges. Gil had been a great player who had known tremendous success as an eight-time All-Star on the legendary Brooklyn Dodgers teams of the late 1940s and 1950s. But during his long career, he had also known defeat. He experienced a major slump on the sport's biggest stage, going hitless in all seven games of the 1952 World Series. He had played on the dismal 120-loss Met team of 1962 and again in 1963. Through all the ups and downs, he comported himself with the same quiet demeanor. For all his baseball acumen, maybe his biggest contribution was in teaching all the young talent in his care how to play like men.

We got better. By Labor Day in that 1968 season, sportswriter Leonard Koppett was able to write in *The New York Times* that, "The Mets, no matter what their final won-loss record will be, have finally turned the corner to respectability." Analyzing our play, Koppett did not spare the criticism. "Tommie Agee, who was supposed to solve center field, didn't. Ron Swoboda, who started fast, went into a three month slump, and is not quite a superstar yet. Bud Harrelson hasn't approached last year's effectiveness. . . . The pitchers, of course, are pure gold. Around such pitchers something can be built. Swoboda, Harrelson, Cleon Jones, Jerry Grote, Ed Kranepool, Ken Boswell may be a nucleus. We'll see."

Yes, we'll see.

Vietnam

That winter, before I laced on another pair of spikes, I did something I thought I would never do. I was asked if I was interested in joining the soon-to-be commissioner of baseball Bowie Kuhn, Joe DiMaggio, and Phillies pitcher Larry Jackson on a USO tour of Vietnam. And instead of returning to the business courses I was taking at NYU, I said yes. DiMaggio, Yankees Hall of Famer, was better known as Mr. Coffee, for the coffeemaker he endorsed on TV, than as "The Greatest Living Ball Player," a moniker he insisted on when introduced at Old Timers events. Jackson had played two decades in the National League, winning 194 games, mostly for the Cubs and Cards. I was the least known.

I did not get off to a good start. At St. Albans Naval Hospital in New York City, a nurse came at me with a set of needles full of enough germs to inoculate me against typhus, malaria, the plague, and who knows what other evils we might encounter in Southeast Asia. She stabbed me with a combination, a shot to each shoulder, but before she could double up on the right side, I went down, knocked out cold. The big tough ballplayer was a sissy when it came to needles.

We flew in a commercial four-engine Boeing 707 airliner chartered by the government, no first class, six abreast, every seat taken.

A graph of U.S. casualties in Vietnam angles up to a point and tapers back down, mirroring the shape of the Vietnam Memorial in Washington, D.C. 1968 would be the peak. We were traveling in late October 1968, and the mood was somber.

Landing at Saigon's Tan Son Nhat Airport after midnight, nervous as hell, we boarded a van, gun jeeps front and behind, and drove pell-mell through the dark avenues of Saigon into the embassy corridor, pulling up at the guard hut in front of the Meyercord Hotel in the Cholon district. In my room waiting for me, I found a pair of jungle boots and a set of olive-green army fatigues with SWOBODA and USO patches above the breast pockets. I later added an American flag patch sewn on my shoulder. My blue-and-orange Mets hat completed the uniform.

Exotic stuff. Here I was in Saigon during a war that was all over television. For three weeks we would travel from the top to the bottom of the country, going everywhere from dinner with General Creighton Abrams at his headquarters to firebases where command would not allow our helicopter to stay on the ground.

The first soufflés I'd ever eaten I enjoyed with General Abrams, commander of all U.S. forces in Vietnam, mere months after he weathered the massive Tet Offensive. With the look and confidence of a CEO, Abrams was the soldier's soldier, comfortable with his visitors. He had been Patton's tank commander, breaking the German encirclement of Bastogne in the Battle of the Bulge. That awed me. It meant more to a good friend in New York, Tom Farone, who had been at Bastogne, cold and low on ammunition.

The talk skimmed the military situation. The general touched on his strategy to back off the firepower, to help "win the hearts and minds" of the South Vietnamese we were fighting for. He likely got that idea from John Paul Vann, written about by Neil Sheehan in his seminal book, *A Bright Shining Lie*. I was fascinated. Abrams, however, seemed more interested in what DiMaggio had to say about baseball. He knew about Joe D's 56-game hitting streak. I got the general to autograph a ball for me. I did mention that we weren't scheduled to visit any marines and had an off-day available. What did we need an off-day for in a three-week visit? His aide-de-camp jumped all over that. When that free day rolled around, a Chinook helicopter scooped us up and delivered us to a Marine general in I Corps, who hustled us to the bases around Da Nang, shaking hands and signing autographs with marines who had some of the shittiest duty in the conflict. They went through mortar-firing drills for us, shelling the nearby hills. I just looked at an old color photo taken of me with a young marine while I was there. He gave it to me during an appearance a couple of years ago at the Empire City Raceway and Casino in Yonkers, New York, one of many people I keep running into who I first met under the gun in Vietnam.

Earlier, we had been in the base hospital wards, talking with soldiers wounded in Tet. One fellow had taken a couple of AK-47 rounds in his upper thigh, and seemed to be doing well. A grenade had blown up close to another soldier whose face was as big as a basketball; he would recover, we were told. Not so with the boy who had 80 percent third-degree burns, though he was talking and seemed reasonably upbeat. That jolted me. But not as much as the young private lying in a bed who asked, "What are you doing here?" When I explained I was an outfielder with the Mets, his face remained blank, underwhelmed. I had nothing for him, and he rolled over and faced the wall. Outside the hospital, a doctor ranted for fifteen minutes about what insanity, what madness, this whole Vietnam thing was. It wasn't anything I hadn't heard a thousand times back home, but hearing it here, from someone so deep into it, left me feeling rattled.

Soldiers came at me from extreme perspectives. A frightened eighteen-year-old who wanted out of all this broke down crying while he handed me his Good Conduct Medal, which hangs on a corkboard in my office. In a field, I met soldiers armed and geared up, tuned up like Valkyries for a helicopter assault. I was walking around when I noticed one trooper with a face out of a high school yearbook, clearly loaded, drunk. The guys with him didn't seem too concerned. One soldier said to me they didn't expect any trouble, asked if I wanted to go along. I had already fired most of the weapons they were carrying: M-16, M-79 grenade launcher, and M-60 belt-fed machine gun in a make-believe war on their garbage dump. My stupid reply: "Sure." I was fired up; the invitation seemed genuine. Fortunately, our escort officer wasn't having any of that. Speaking with civilian casualness, a combat veteran, maybe in his late twenties, described a U-shaped ambush his guys had just executed where he fed six magazines, flawlessly, through his M-16, wasting the enemy. Good news, since the weapon's early models in the war were extremely problematic with jams and such.

And then there were the Green Berets, who might have been fucking with us. We traveled to the Green Beret camp up a narrow canal in a Boston Whaler with an outboard motor and a Browning belt-fed .30 machine gun guy mounted in the bow. Larry Jackson mentioned that he'd hunted mule deer in Idaho, so a noncom handed him a loaded M-16 and gave him a quick lesson in using it. We were cruising along past a village that suddenly seemed vacant. A wide fishing net draped across the water blocked our progress. The machine gunner charged a round with a metallic *cha-chink*, and said, "Heads up!" I knew what that meant because we used the same expression in baseball, but it never made my heart beat like this. My brain flash was that if the shit hit the fan, I'm rolling into this canal and staying there, trying not to be dead. A villager appeared and lifted the fishing net, and we proceeded to the camp.

Larry Jackson was our official photographer. Most of the Super 8 stuff he shot was out of focus. Damn. All the footage I shot with my movie camera has disappeared. Double damn.

The Green Berets invited us into their *last ditch bunker,* a reinforced concrete redoubt sheathed with chain-link fencing designed to defend against warheads armed with shaped explosive charges. Inside they kept enough weapons and ammunition to turn Custer's Last Stand into a victory. What they called the coup de grâce was a steel tube extending straight out the roof for firing mortars. If worse came to worst, the campground attacked and overrun, they could rain mortar rounds right on top of themselves. They were serious.

This was not. With DiMaggio and Bowie Kuhn, we dropped in on an artillery firebase featuring 155mm self-propelled howitzers emplaced in pits ringed by high dirt berms. While they were shooting off white phosphorus shells for calibration and range finding, we got permission to climb the berms to watch the crews working the big guns. The flash control devices on the muzzles deflected gases powerfully sideways. As Kuhn came over the berm, a cannon fired. The blast caught him full and knocked him backward. Mr. Coffee and I watched the usually ramrod-straight, soon-to-be commissioner of baseball rolling ass over tin cups down to meet us at the bottom. We all laughed. I don't think I ever forgot to mention Bowie's great fall to Joe D. on the occasions we were together in the future. Joe never forgot it, either.

I was delighted to see Martha Raye, the singer-comedienne and star from movies and television, walk into the Meyercord, a case of Smirnoff vodka for her and her beloved Green Berets stowed with her suitcases and gear. Where she was going she wouldn't say, for security reasons. Her ride was with Air America, operated by the CIA, the worst-kept secret in Vietnam, in their shiny, silver airplanes and helicopters that stood out like nightclub marquees. Martha did everything in her power to champion the Green Berets, whatever they needed. She had an Army Reserve commission, a full-bird colonel. A registered nurse specializing in field surgery, she wore the caduceus emblem on her army fatigues. Martha served in the battle zones, treating the wounded. She earned a Purple Heart for wounds received under fire, which she made light of. Totally worthy, far more than a USO entertainer, she is the only woman buried in the Green Beret cemetery at Fort Bragg.

Joey Bishop showed up around the same time. One of Frank Sinatra's Rat Pack, a stand-up comedian and TV star in his own right, Bishop had paid his own way to entertain the troops with his Vegas revue on a tour separate from ours. I have a wonderful picture on my office wall of all of us sitting around the common room in the hotel, Martha, me, Joey playing mandolin, and someone else on guitar, enjoying one another's company in the midst of this horrible war. After our Series win in '69, I got a call from Joey while we were celebrating upstairs at Shea Stadium, and we talked live on his radio show, sharing a few thoughts from our time together in Vietnam.

I would be back in Vietnam again the following year when I would spend some time with a special guy I still talk to, Craig Lang. He's the son of the late sportswriter, Jack. I had met Craig as a kid with his dad at Shea. Jack let me know where I might find his son in Vietnam. He was with the infantry in the central highlands around An Khe, which by chance was a stop on our tour. I arrived there in one of the ever-present Huey helicopters, accompanied by Mudcat Grant, a well-traveled pitcher who had played for Cleveland, Minnesota, and many other clubs. He was a Black Ace, one of the African American 20-game winners that he eventually wrote a book about.

I asked some officers if they could connect me with Craig. It happened that the executive officer of his unit was standing there. He knew right where to send the helicopter to scoop Craig out of the jungle. I was drinking, probably a double martini, in the officers' club. In walks Craig looking like hell. With rotting boots and the gray jungle pallor he got from living under triple canopy, Craig wore a nonregulation camo kerchief around his neck like Eli Wallach in *The Good, the Bad and the Ugly*. That drew some attention from the brass as Craig and I sat down for a surf-and-turf dinner. Other than Craig, a specialist fourth class, and a light corporal, the only swinging dick ranked below a major was the captain escorting our tour. After dinner and more than a few drinks, Craig's military bearing let down even more, and it seemed like a good time for us to leave.

So we went over to the Sergeant's Club and continued the evening. At sunset, in possession of superior buzzes, we rode up the hill to the bachelor officers' quarters where we would sleep that night. Getting out of the jeep, I looked back down the road to see and hear a sharp explosion near the command post at the front gate, then another blast not far from where we just left. The Vietcong were firing RPG rockets, which proved a diversion straight out of Sun Tzu's book on warfare. Jesus, talk about taking the edge off your buzz. I can't remember sobering up any quicker. Sirens went off as An Khe went on alert. We were corralled into the underground command bunker. I had a .38 pistol in my pocket, but nobody quoted me Mae West's famous line. Once it was obvious we weren't being ground-attacked, we sat on the top of the bunker. The focus had been the helicopter pad. Sappers had tossed satchel charges up against nineteen helicopters, and one by one we watched the explosions and the choppers' magnesium-aluminum skin light up the night.

A C-47 gunship, a Spooky, with the otherworldish *brrrrrbrrrr brrrr* moan of its Gatling gun, started working the perimeter of the base, hosing down the jungle with a solid string of red-hot tracers. I was told one GI was killed by a satchel charge thrown up against his wooden barracks. When things quieted down, I went with Mudcat and Craig to the MASH unit. A soldier wounded in the attack couldn't speak, and his eyes were bandaged. They told us he would hear us. Not sure of that at all, but we put as many positives in his ear as we could. Years later, Mudcat told me that this soldier connected with him in St. Louis, saying, "I could hear you guys," and thanked him for being there. A couple of years ago, I went to Mudcat Grant's charity golf tournament in Binghamton, New York, and met another GI, who we first encountered at the guard post outside the Meyercord in Saigon.

3

1969

Looking back over those fifty years, nearing my seventy-fifth birthday, 1969 seems Dickensian: it was the best of times for some and the very worst of times for others. Souls were being tried by the struggles over the Vietnam War and the civil rights movement. The year before, 1968, witnessed the crushing murders of Martin Luther King Jr. and Bobby Kennedy, two champions of peace and justice; meanwhile the death toll in Vietnam peaked at nearly seventeen thousand. In terms of spectacle, however, 1969 did manage to feature the unparalleled astrophysical triumph of landing two men on the moon, and then, just about a month later, landing a half million people on Max Yasgur's farm in upstate New York for a music festival forever immortalized as Woodstock. From outer space to spaced out, 1969 had it all, due in large part to a war economy surging amidst a cultural stew where everything seemed possible.

I cannot imagine a more compelling time to be young in America if you had money, a good job, and a draft deferment. I had all three. My job was chasing fly balls for the New York Mets at $34,000 a year, more than four times the salary of the average American. My deferment was named Cecilia, still my wife after almost fifty-four years, who blessed me with an enduring marriage and two sons, Ron Jr. and Brian. Like Swoboda is freedom in Polish, in America, in 1969, I had the freedom to at least try to be the best baseball player I could be.

In the chill of a Long Island January, the new year rolled around and with it a more urgent sense of drive. I would be twenty-five years old in the coming season, the Mets had won 73 games the year before, and I had led them with 59 RBIs. It felt like I was at the peak of my potential ability to perform, and it was time to get serious about conditioning, to mix in some sprints and jogging around my Long Island neighborhood of Syosset, increase those push-ups, pull-ups, and sit-ups I'd been doing in the basement. All that, plus swinging a bat at a tire hanging from a rope in my backyard (I never missed it), was the extent of my workouts. I never used weights and never went to a gym to work out, ever. Now, I chunk around all kinds of weights to help my golf swing. As a former physical education major, I should have known better.

I loved the spring. Who doesn't love spring? (Penguins and snowmen get no vote here.) The clocks move forward every spring, but my mind moves backward toward golden memories as a kid growing up in Sparrows Point. When nature blessed us in April, my Mom's tulips started poking their noses up out of the beds around the house, competing with our forsythia bushes busy exploding with yellow blossoms.

Caring about the spring, knowing it was special, led me, in an almost seamless single file, into being paid to play a game whose annual renewal is called spring training. Hard to appreciate at the time, but that burst of energy, that quickening of the pulse, that sense of rebirth, wanting to believe that you could make the coming year better than the last was deeply ingrained in me. It's such a beguiling, beneficent delusion, encouraging artists, composers, and poets to overpraise that time of year. As Emily Dickinson wrote, "A little Madness in the Spring is wholesome even for the King."

Listen online to Aaron Copland's *Appalachian Spring,* and tell me if it doesn't sound like what I'm trying to say.

Copland's *Appalachian Spring,* certainly, could have been the soundtrack to several Februarys in the late 1960s, as Cecilia and I packed our two boys and our big black dog, Waggles, into a large Buick station wagon for the road trip south to Florida. We loaded our roof rack with two large Samsonite suitcases and a bunch of our other junk crammed into every square inch up top. That gave us ample space inside the car as we rumbled down the road looking remarkably like the Wagon Queen Family Truckster vehicle created for those very funny Chevy Chase National Lampoon vacation movies in the 1980s. With the roof rack full, Waggles had the backseat to himself, and the two boys could stretch out into what we called the way back, watching the highway out the tailgate window.

Our kids, RJ (Ron Jr.) and Brian, were great travelers, staying busy with Etch A Sketch, cards, books, or invented games involving the numbers on passing license plates. We traveled well, coordinating our kidneys with our gas stops. At about the halfway point in our journey, usually near Charleston, South Carolina, we spent the night. Friends of my parents, Ted and Ann Kurik, lived on Isle of Palms, and put us up. Ted worked in quality control at the naval base in Charleston where they refueled nuclear submarines, kind of a hush-hush job that he couldn't talk much about.

Completely lost on me at the time was their proximity to Fort Sumter, in Charleston harbor, where a Creole French Confederate general from New Orleans, P. G. T. Beauregard, commanded the troops that fired the first shots in the Civil War. I later learned that the second-in-command of the federal troops inside the fort during the bombardment was Captain, later General, Abner Doubleday, who for many years was falsely credited with inventing the game of baseball. The complete fabrication had been orchestrated by A. G. Spalding, who had been a player, team owner, organizer of the National League, original rule-writer, and sporting goods entrepreneur. Evidently, he wanted to separate baseball from its historical roots in rounders, a game popular with girls in Britain. No one had more fun with this stray fact than the late Red Smith, one of our best sportswriters ever, who would often refer to the World Series in his column in *The New York Times* as the Rounders Championships of North America. Arrogance and pomposity were his favorite bubbles to burst.

With our station wagon full of Swobodas and Waggles, we rolled into St. Petersburg, Florida, in late February, and headed directly for Pass-a-Grille Beach, and the house we rented for spring training. Cecilia would handle the kids, as my mind locked onto baseball. The team played mostly day games after morning workouts, so, until our two kids were in school, me, Cecilia, and the whole family headed south and lived a nine-to-five existence, like regular people. Some of my favorite times, ever. I loved having dinner with my gang, and then catching nighttime TV shows like *Bonanza, Gilligan's Island, Mission: Impossible,* and *The Ed Sullivan Show*. Little did I dream that many months in the future, one of the perks for our good work in 1969 would be an appearance on Ed's show. We were also fans of old movies, particularly the ones starring Jerry Lewis. Many years later, I met Jerry at a golf course in Phoenix, just hanging out, hitting some balls. When I told him that I liked all of them, even the drama *The King of Comedy*, he said, "So you're the one." I prize the ball I have with his autograph on it.

In 1969, Major League Baseball celebrated the centennial of its creation, and also marked a spring of sweeping change. As the popularity of the National Football League surged, enthusiasm for the National Pastime leveled off. One suspect was diminishing offense. In 1968, hitting dropped off dramatically. Pitchers ruled, throwing 339 shutouts during the year. Denny McLain of the Tigers won 31 games, the first to win 30 since Dizzy Dean in 1934. Bob Gibson posted a 1.12 earned run average, the lowest in fifty-four years. The best hitters in baseball cranked out a measly eight hits in the National League's 1–0 victory in the All-Star Game. In the American League, only one player, Boston's Carl Yastrzemski, managed to finish the season with a batting average higher than .300. (The National League was better, but still, only five players surmounted .300.) Once the powers that be became convinced that low scores translated into low attendance, big league baseball lowered the mound about a half a foot, taking away some of the pitcher's leverage. They even toyed with introducing a livelier baseball.

They also added four teams: the San Diego Padres and Montreal Expos in the National League, and the Seattle Pilots and Kansas City Royals in the American League. (After a year, the Pilots moved to Milwaukee and became the Brewers, and after a much longer run, the Expos moved to Washington and became the Nationals.) Expansion is always novel and stirs up interest, but the bigger change this time was the decision to add playoffs. For that first century, the two teams that ended baseball's long slog of a season with the best record were the league champions; now the leagues split into two divisions, East and West, each with six teams. The first place finishers in each division would then face each other for the league championship, and the right to advance to the World Series.

But progress never comes without controversy. Marvin Miller, formerly of the Steelworkers Union, just two years into his role as executive director of the Major League Baseball Players Association, calculated that with four new teams and another layer in the playoffs creating more TV money, the MLB owners should, rightfully, up their annual contribution to the players' pension fund. The issue was settled when the players executed a job action delaying spring training a few days until the owners, with a brand-new commissioner in Bowie Kuhn, fumbling through moths and cob-webs, finally loosened up the purse strings for the few extra bucks that got big league training camps opened on February 25.

Sunny as the weather may have been, the Mets opened camp with concerns, including a big one at the top. In September of 1968, in Atlanta, our manager Gil Hodges, wrapping up his first year, suffered what was characterized as a mild heart attack. I've never met anyone tougher than Hodges, whose service in the Marine Corps during World War II included fighting in the Battle of Okinawa. During the winter, Gil dropped twenty-five pounds and quit a two-pack-a-day cigarette habit, earning him a medical okay to attend spring training. The sportswriter George Vecsey asked what would have happened if he had received a less favorable diagnosis. Hodges replied, "I'd change doctors, that's all." Those were serious words from a marine who knew exactly what it looked like to die with your boots on.

Today, even nearing the age of seventy-five, my failure to get along with Gil Hodges when I was playing for him sits like a stone in my gut. Of all the opportunities I blew, in a life full of them, botching the relationship with Hodges is the stupidest thing I ever did. Hodges was all about playing the game the right way, conducting yourself like a mature adult and helping the team win games. Period. That's all he wanted from me, and I couldn't fucking deliver it.

Even as I write this, I'm not entirely sure where the explanations lie. You didn't have to watch Gil operate very long to come to a couple of obvious conclusions. This man had a clear idea what he was trying to do as a manager. He had a quick mind and the game never, ever got ahead of him. He could be creative when the situation arose, and his solutions seemed to resolve themselves in a way that we lesser lights could understand. If, say, the home team was batting with the bases loaded in the bottom of the ninth, he might bring in a fifth infielder and let the pitcher try to throw a ground ball. Once he brought me in from right field to play first base while the rest of the infielders charged a pitcher who was looking to bunt while we dared him to swing the bat. We platooned a lot with those 1968 and '69 Met teams, but he would also go with his gut when it spoke to him. He let me hit against sidearming right-hander Eddie Watt in Game Five of the 1969 World Series with the winning run on and a good left-handed hitter in Art Shamsky on the bench. Fortunately, I made both of us look good.

There were other things, though. Hodges was with the Marines in World War II, which I did know, and on Okinawa for that awful string of battles, which I did not know. It might have made a difference. It was something he never talked about. His son, Gilly, told me once that his Dad sat him down and gave him the short, ugly story of Okinawa and never brought it up again. Somebody once said that Gil's smile was "more muscular than merry," a phrase that seems pretty on the nose to me. I wonder if that was true before the Marine Corps. I learned only last year that before Gil traveled to Okinawa, he spent time on Tinian in the Marianas. Gil left Tinian in early March, 1945, while my Dad showed up on Tinian in late March with his B-29 crew and was there until the end of the war.

Most of what Gil was thinking was revealed in what he did. He kept what he was feeling, his emotions, locked tightly inside—right next to those awful memories of fighting on Okinawa. Tom Seaver, who served eight years in the Marine Reserves between 1962 and 1970, once asked Hodges about Okinawa. All Gil said was, "If you want to know what it was like, you needed to be there."

I've always had a problem with authority. As a kid it seemed that whatever the problem was, my feelings about it weren't considered important, and I found that difficult to accept. Even today, I bristle when I am told what to do. It seems clear to me now that all Gil wanted from us was to act like we had a brain and be the best player we could be. Back then, I couldn't get past the instinct to push back. I remember when we opened the 1968 season in Pittsburgh. It was Gil's first as our manager, and he called a meeting, supposedly to let us set curfew, the time we would have to be in the hotel after a game. As he put it, "You guys are going to have to live with it, so you guys decide." Somebody said something like, "Three hours after the game." And Gil said, "No, that's too late." My big mouth chimed in with, "Why don't you just tell us what time you want it to be and get this over with?" It was brash of me to open my mouth that way, but the thing is, they agreed with me. Nobody objected to a curfew; it was the discussion that seemed to be a waste of time, and the guys were glad that somebody was stupid enough to open his yap. Today I am amazed that I would have said that; after all, there's a logic to curfews. When I played for the Montreal Expos, Gene Mauch, the best manager not in the Hall of Fame other than Hodges, set a curfew and enforced it, saying, "I want 100 percent of what you got. Not 100 percent of what's left." Point taken. But Gil did have a way of making the true path he wanted us to follow feel a little narrow. Once a couple of us went to a Western store in Houston and bought cowboy hats. Mine was a $50 7X Stetson, which was a pretty good hat. Gil greeted us when we got on the airplane sporting our new lids. "You boys enjoy those hats today," he said. "You won't be wearing them tomorrow." Whether we thought that had anything to do with us being a good baseball team or not, the marine had spoken and that was that.

Hodges's health would be good for the coming season, but the larger question in camp, far more significant, was the matter of whether we would be any good. In the Mets' seven years of existence, the club had finished 10th, 10th, 10th, 10th, 9th, 10th, and 9th. In 1968, we had set the team record for victories, going 73–89, and yet we still finished 24 games behind the St. Louis Cardinals.

I think we expected to be better—hey, with divisional play, we weren't going to finish worse than sixth!—but I didn't feel any manifest destiny. We had pitchers for sure. Tom Seaver and Jerry Koosman had won 35 games between them in 1968, and when you threw Tug McGraw, Gary Gentry, Nolan Ryan, and Jim McAndrew into the mix, I'm not really sure anybody in Major League Baseball was as blessed as we were with as many good, young, hard throwers who could also pitch. (As most of you know, there is a difference between throwing and pitching. Lots of guys can hump the ball up to the plate in the mid-to-upper 90s; pitching—the mental part, the control part—requires intelligence, craft, and even a bit of artistry.) The Mets' problem was hitting. In a year when all hitting was down, we were nearly the bottom of the barrel; in 1968, we scored the second fewest runs in all of baseball.

Hodges fingered 85 wins as a very achievable goal for 1969. Whether he really thought that we could reach that total or not we'll never know, but I don't believe that a former marine would waste time setting an easily obtainable goal. Most of the preseason prognosticators were picking us for third place, rare air for perennial bottom dwellers. Even our leader, George Thomas Seaver, was aiming high. "The supreme optimist says we'll finish second in the Eastern Division of the league," Tom told *The New York Times*. "The only team we can't catch is St. Louis. The only other team we might have to fight off is Chicago. But we can beat Pittsburgh, Philadelphia, and Montreal. Who's the supreme optimist? Me."

I guess that's the way most everybody saw it—we could play with anybody except the Cards. Led by Bob Gibson, they had won the NL title in three of the last five seasons and gone on to win the World Series two of those three times. What was clear was that if we were to start contending, we would need more thump in the lineup. I had led the regular starters in 1967 with a .281 batting average, and in 1968 with 59 RBIs. With those numbers, no one was going to quake when the Mighty Mets rolled into town. We needed more hitting.

On a spring training visit to West Palm Beach in 1969, the Mets opened talks with Paul Richards, the GM of the Atlanta Braves and a canny judge of talent. The Braves had a lot of hitting but nobody ever had enough pitching, and Richards was dangling Joe Torre, a twenty-eight-year-old catcher/first baseman from Brooklyn who had twice driven in more than 100 runs and had the potential to do it again. Richards wanted to get his mitts on our young pitchers, guys like Ryan or McAndrew or Koosman. The names of young hitters, Ed Kranepool and Amos Otis, popped up as well. But Johnny Murphy, the Mets GM, had Otis, Koosman, Seaver, catcher Jerry Grote, shortstop Bud Harrelson, outfielder Cleon Jones, and yours truly on a list of "untouchables." "I never knew the Mets had so many untouchables," the frustrated Richards griped. "I'm surprised they didn't win the pennant." That was a good line. I wonder if he was still laughing when we swept the Braves in the first ever N.L.C.S.

When talks broke down, Murphy took some heat for it from Dick Young, an influential columnist for the *Daily News*, who thought Torre would have made the Mets a contender. He wasn't necessarily wrong; in 1969 Joe would knock in over 100 runs again (and would win the Most Valuable Player Award in 1971), but whether or not we would have contended depended on who had been subtracted in the deal. What it says to me, looking back over a lot of years now, is that Murphy, a onetime pitcher himself, really didn't see us as contenders just yet. He, and I suppose Hodges, too, was willing to open the season with a couple of youthful, unproven, inconsistent position players, while our young power arms continued to develop. We ain't soup yet, so keep it over a low heat and keep your eyes on it. Today, modern medicine can do some amazing things with pitchers, but then and even now, young pitching is a vital commodity. You never want to give any of it up. With Met fans showing patience, the high command figured they could play their cards close. Stand pat but watch the pot.

Meanwhile, spring training in St. Petersburg proceeded as it always did. You would go out in week one and hit and throw, and with no sunscreen available, your skin would burn and peel and then tan, if it could. Meanwhile, no matter how much work you had done running and stretching, you were going to run and stretch some more, to the point that you would start to hurt in places you never had before. Finally, things would settle down for the position players into days of practice and more practice. I loved getting lost in the wonderful Zen of practice, how one day repeated the one before; it was very relaxing. By the time we reached the last two weeks, the Zen wore off, and the position players were bored to tears. We were ready, because the only reason spring training lasted as long as it did was to get the starting pitchers stretched out and the rotation organized.

Back then, for a starting pitcher, getting ready meant getting ready to pitch nine innings, to throw 120 pitches, or more, if needed, hard and accurately. The coaching staff nursed our abundance of young arms with kid gloves and motherly love that was never evident for us hitters. "We were second-class citizens," says eighteen-year veteran New York Met Ed Kranepool. Today, big league teams have two hitting coaches, a wealth of video to study, analysts measuring the trajectory of every swing. Back then, we had none of that, and that was too bad. As Eddie explains, "You need someone watching you when you're going good and when you're going bad. You can't tell if your hands are moving into the wrong place. You need somebody watching you." True, we had the immortal Yogi Berra on our coaching staff, but among Yogi's many baseball gifts, coaching hitting wasn't one. Analysis wasn't Yogi's strong suit. During all those years when he and the Yankees were routinely chalking up World Series titles, Yogi never had a stance nor for that matter a strike zone. All he did was hit. It was said that Yogi was a good bad ball hitter and a better good ball hitter, but he couldn't coach hitting. Yogi told me once, "If you can't hit it, don't swing at it." And I said, "What about with two strikes?" Yogi said, with all the clarity he could muster, "Well, then, you might have to swing at it." And that's the way it went.

On the upside, Cleon Jones, our left fielder, was teaching himself the mechanics of hitting. His roots in Mobile, Alabama, made it well aware that his hometown had already produced a couple of big-time hitters destined for the Hall of Fame in the Braves' Hank Aaron, Willie McCovey—who just passed in late 2018—and the Cubs' Billy Williams. The year before, Cleon had hit a solid .297 with 14 home runs and twice as many doubles. Unlike me, he was figuring it out. He would sit in a little room we had with 16mm film loops of our at bats, and study himself. "I got to the point where I could do what I wanted with the bat," Cleon was telling me. "I concentrated on hitting line drives. I thought I could get two or three hits every game. My thing was to hit .300." He'd do better than that in 1969 with a career high .340, competing for the National League batting title that Pete Rose won hitting .348. Even with all that, Cleon, like yours truly, would, inevitably, work his way into Gil Hodges's shithouse.

Before we were very deep into spring training, a writer asked Gil if he believed in platooning. "I do for this team," was his reply. Platooning players, for the uninitiated, means using players in part-time roles that make the most of what they can do well and minimize what they struggle with. "I try to put my players in a position to succeed, not in a position to fail," explained Earl Weaver, the famous manager of the Orioles who platooned frequently. Usually in a platoon, a right-handed hitter will start against left-handed pitchers, and vice versa. As spring training went by, Hodges showed that he planned to use a lot of combinations. That's an understatement; Cleon Jones in left and Tommie Agee in center ended up being the only players Gil didn't regularly platoon. In my case, that meant sharing right field with the left-hand-hitting Art Shamsky. Three years older than me, a native of St. Louis, and a product of the Cincinnati organization, Art, from the left side, was a better hitter for average than me, so I couldn't beef about it, but I wanted to play every day. I wanted to believe if I got the at bats, I would adjust to right-handed pitching, and produce better numbers. But the truth is, Hodges was right. If you looked at our combined performance, Sham and I ended up being like a 100 RBI guy in right field, even though we lived in two different places and drove two different cars to the ballpark. It wasn't what either of us wanted, but it was the way Hodges was going, and over time, all of the fellows bought into Gil's plan. One reason is that day in and day out, Gil was as creative a manager as I had ever seen. His mind was always churning with things that might improve his options as a manager. Shamsky had played a little bit of first base with the Reds before coming our way and Gil had him working out there. Cleon Jones was also taking some turns around first base. I had made a run at that position back in 1967, before Hodges, who had won three Gold Gloves at that position, took over as manager. (If you ever saw Gil's hands, you'd know why he was such a great first baseman—they were enormous.) It only took about twenty games for me to convince everyone what a bad idea it was. But Sham could play the position and things went fine—up to a point.

"A couple of games into spring training, I was taking throws from Bozzy"—second baseman Kenny Boswell—"when I felt something painful in my left lower back," Sham said. So he took a little rubdown from our trainer, Gus Mauch, and then went to the game at Al Lang Field. There the pain got worse. "I felt like somebody shot me in my left hip." Gus was a longtime trainer who had worked with the New York Football Giants and the championship Yankee teams of the 1950s. He came into the profession as a masseur, trained as a chiropractor, and certainly knew as much about sports injuries as anyone in pro sports. In today's world, Sham would have immediately gone for an MRI; based on the images, the training staff and doctors would have put their heads together and decided on a course of action, which might include any number of sophisticated surgical techniques. Back then, Sham was sent to a local doctor in St. Pete who took an X-ray. He concluded that Sham had disturbed a disc in his back that had impinged on his sciatic nerve, and put him on bed rest. That was it.

"For about three weeks, I took all my meals in bed," Sham said. "Nobody supervised my rehab." After twenty-one days of bed rest, the pain subsided and Sham started stretching and jogging. Grudgingly he started the season at the Mets' AAA club at Tidewater. His first appearance for the Mets wouldn't come until May 13, when he pinch hit against the Braves.

With Sham on the shelf, I figured I would inherit his at bats and right field would be mine, at least in the early going. But a couple of things derailed my thinking. Statistically, I had a flat-assed awful spring, while a twenty-three-year-old rookie, Rod Gaspar, emerged. I'm like, "Who the hell is this?" Rod may not have been as surprised as I was. "In '68 I led the Texas League with 160 base hits, but they didn't even know who I was." That all changed when Gaspar, a switch-hitting, very solid defensive outfielder with some speed and a good arm, lit up the spring with an eye-opening fourteen-game hitting streak. One of the easiest things to overvalue is a spring training batting average, but Gaspar cracked the Mets' Opening Day roster, joining another rookie outfielder, Amos Otis, also from Mobile, Alabama, who was just twenty-two and an even brighter prospect. The rub with Otis was that Hodges wanted him to embrace a shift from the outfield to third base, and Amos made it clear he wanted nothing to do with it.

After the season, this led to a chain reaction of unfortunate events. The Mets traded the unhappy Otis to the Kansas City Royals, where he immediately blossomed into an All-Star Gold Glove outfielder who played fourteen solid seasons in K.C. In return, the Mets got my winter baseball buddy, Joe Foy, a New York City native who tragically reconnected with some bad elements from his youth that led to his addiction to drugs. Joe was gone from the Mets after one season, out of baseball after two, and dead of a heart attack at age forty-six. While that trade was bad enough, it is not considered the worst deal in Mets franchise history. However, it led to the worst one. After the 1971 season, the Mets decided they needed to replace Foy, so they committed another mega-miscue when they traded Nolan Ryan and a couple of other players to the California Angels for Jim Fregosi, a former All-Star on his last legs. Imagine: in those two deals, the Mets squandered two cornerstone players for . . . nothing.

Spring training finally drew to a close. The wives and families were left to make their own way north. Cecilia was very close with Sharon Grote, then the lovely wife of our starting catcher, Jerry Grote. In an age before smartphones, Cecilia and Sharon caravanned their vehicles loaded with kids and dogs up the East Coast about twelve hundred miles back to the Big Apple, on their own. (It must have been a special experience; Sharon and Cecilia have remained close friends.) Meanwhile, we big, badass players would do the team thing. We were like little boys in the bubble. We would get on the team bus to take us to the team-chartered flight back to New York where we would team up in the clubhouse at Shea Stadium, or to some other city where we would stay at the team-reserved hotel.

But what sort of team would we be? Young, surely: we had been young the year before, and we were still young. Smart: twenty-one of the twenty-five guys had some college to their credit. Talented: sure, at least to some degree. But were we good? Obviously, the front office had no expectations that we would be playing ball in October. They sent us to war with two rookies in the outfield and three unproven infielders: Wayne Garrett, a twenty-one-year-old rookie, plus Ken Boswell and Kevin Collins, who among them had played a smattering of games across five major league seasons without amassing twenty RBIs. Management probably believed that the pieces were coming together, but they didn't see a need to rush things. I think the players thought we'd be better. "I was hoping for improvement," my old roommate, Ed Kranepool, recalled recently on the phone. Cleon Jones agreed. "Guys were coming of age and the leadership improved with Gil Hodges and those great arms." But spring training ended, and the high command stood pat. The message we received seemed clear: you are more than a move or two away.

In March, shortly before we broke camp, the 11th Grammy Awards honored Roy Halee, my neighbor in Syosset, Long Island, who was engineer/producer on Simon and Garfunkel's Record of the Year, "Mrs. Robinson." Roy had actually tried to buy our house before Cecilia and I snagged it. Somehow in the process, we became good friends. His kids played with ours, and through him we got to meet Paul Simon and Art Garfunkel. "Mrs. Robinson," their tune featured in *The Graduate*, went to number one on the charts, and is famous for asking, "Where have you gone, Joe DiMaggio?" Perhaps this was Paul Simon's reference to the loss of grace in our culture. When Joe and I visited Vietnam together, the song was never out of my head.

On the shelf in my office today are two baseballs. One, from the

1994 World Series (the W.S. that wasn't because of a job action by the players and owners), bears the question, no longer rhetorical, "Where have you gone Joe DiMaggio?" Signed by Paul Simon. The other big league ball, in a hand as graceful as Joe's gait, says, "I haven't gone anywhere." Signed by Joe D.

The Games Begin

April 8, 1969. It's Opening Day. Shea Stadium was decked out in its finest red-white-and-blue bunting on a cool, clear day humming with anticipation. With temperatures in the mid-50s, perfect for long sleeves and a jacket, especially if you're sitting on the bench, like I was. There was always the expression that spring training stats are written in pencil; on Opening Day, they start using ink. Gil Hodges wrote the lineup in ink, and my name wasn't in it.

In the front row of the box seats off the right end of our dugout sat Mrs. Joan Whitney Payson, the team owner, wearing her blue and orange Mets colors. She was technically co-owner with her brother, "Jock" Whitney, who at various times had been the U.S. ambassador to the United Kingdom, publisher of the *New York Herald Tribune*, president of the Museum of Modern Art, owner of a racing stable, and a highly regarded polo player. (He made the cover of *Time* magazine in 1933 for his prowess in polo.) We rarely saw him. Her husband, a Wall Street financier from a prominent Maine family, was Charles Shipman Payson, who cared about baseball even less than Jock. We didn't see him much, either. Mrs. Payson was a large, spirited woman who grew up loving art, racehorses, and the New York Giants. Through M. Donald Grant, her money guy, she invested that emotion and about $5 million in the Mets. Grant was chairman of the board. The joke was that the difference between the Whitneys and the Paysons was that the Paysons knew how much money they had. As wealthy as she was, our sense was that Ms. Joan cared deeply about the team and the players. Cecilia and I still have two silver cups from Tiffany's in New York, gifted to us to celebrate the birth of each of our sons. The team had yet to gift Mrs. Payson with an Opening Day win, a string running to seven seasons.

You had to like our chances on this Opening Day with our ace Seaver on the bump against the expansion Montreal Expos. And if I told you that we would get 15 hits and score 10 runs, you'd run over your children to get somewhere you could put some money on us. Well, the abundant bunting and 44,500 fans all went for naught as Seaver flopped, getting roughed up in five innings of work for six hits and four runs. The rest of the staff offered no help, as the Expos put up four runs in the top of the eighth and spoiled our home opener with an 11–10 win. Hodges used seventeen players. Young, switch-hitting Rod Gaspar, Gil's hot hand out of spring training, went 2-for-5, drove in a run, and scored once. I pinch hit in the seventh with one out and runners at first and second, the tying run in scoring position, and promptly slammed into a classic 5–4–3 inning-ending double play and resumed my spot on the bench before my seat got cool.

Game two in 1969 was its own kind of weird, and if what you wanted to do was watch, I had a good seat again, in the dugout. Our young righty, Jim McAndrew, faltered early, but Tug McGraw, in a stopper roll, strung together 6.1 innings of middle relief and we won 9–5. What's weird about that? Well, the save went to Nolan Ryan. Quickie quiz. In his twenty-seven-year Hall of Fame career, how many saves did Nolan Ryan have? Answer: three, which happens to be the same number of runs right fielder Rod Gaspar scored in his second major league start. Adding to that two hits in three tries. Gaspar was going good, and my ass was getting sore. I'm thinking . . . hmmm . . . would you like a little stomach acid with your coffee? This is how a player who is "untouchable" during the pre-season ends up calling Mayflower movers and getting fit for another team's uni.

Outside the bubble, the U.S. had just announced "Vietnamiza-tion," beginning to turn the war effort over to the South Vietnamese Mandarin Catholics, who couldn't handle the country in the first place. With our KIAs close to a thousand a month, huge antiwar demonstrations broke out all over the nation. Interesting because the soundtrack for all this, the billboard tops in pop music, was a bunch of sweet nothings like "Crimson and Clover," by Tommy James and the Shondells. Or as my oldest son pronounced it, "Qwim-son an Qwover." That speech thing matured. The 5th Dimension hit around then with "Aquarius/Let the Sun Shine." John Lennon and his new wife, Yoko Ono, released in early July the only authentic protest song, "Give Peace a Chance," recorded during their Bed-In for Peace in a hotel room in Montreal where they seemed forever in their jammies. Our top movies had more bite to them with Sam Peckinpah's *The Wild Bunch,* a bloody shoot-'em-up. Paul Newman and Robert Redford met their end as *Butch Cassidy and the Sun-dance Kid.* (The Sundance Film Festival was now Redford's baby.) *Midnight Cowboy* showed the bitter streets of New York and came out with an X-rating. (Probably PG today.) Dustin Hoffman was Ratso Rizzo, in the crosswalk screaming at a New York cabbie, "I'm walking here, I'm walking here," while the city eats him alive.

Back inside the baseball bubble, I finally got the nod to start in game three, in left field. It was windy and rainy, temps in the mid-50s. Gil went with his all-right-handed lineup, with Cleon Jones moving in to play first base against the Expos' veteran lefty Larry Jaster. The year before, Jaster, then pitching for the Cardinals against the Mets, came within four outs of a perfect game, his string of re-tired batters broken up when Greg Goossen singled. That day I drove in our first run, Tommie Agee touched up Jaster for two solo bombs, and we won 4–2. A few days later, on April 14, when the Expos played their home opener in Parc Jarry in Montreal, Jaster would be granted the honor of throwing the first major league pitch in the first major league game in Canadian history. Chased in the fourth, Jaster developed shoulder problems and was out of baseball the following year.

Like Jaster, our fearless rookie right-hander, Gary Gentry, would see his own career shortened by arm problems. Joining the Mets from Arizona State, the school Roger Angell dubbed the Notre Dame of college baseball, Gentry pitched with power and movement on his heater, and became the only Met in 1969 to win his first two starts. Gent, who came from Phoenix, always seemed to have a lot of cowboy in him. He was the kind of guy who appeared glad to be around you, and just as happy and maybe happier when he wasn't. After baseball, Gent became a troubling enigma; something of a loner at heart, now, hard to find. In Gent's first win, your boy went 2-for-3, driving in the first Met run. Gaspar took an 0-for-4. No gloating here. I never rooted against Rod; I wanted us to win, and I wanted to play. Besides, he wasn't writing the lineup card.

Gaspar, who told me he played handball for conditioning in the off-season, rebounded in game four with three base hits, one of them a double against the Cardinals' future Hall of Fame left-hander Steve Carlton. I also collected a pair of knocks, but Koosman was a little imprecise and took the loss.

On April 12, the old in and out continued, and I got to watch as the Cards' Dave Giusti shut us out on a six-hitter. Gasper sucked up an 0-for-4 but still clung to the right field spot. Then came Mister Bob Gibson.

I never had to struggle for an answer to the question most asked of me by baseball fans: Bob Gibson was, by far, the toughest pitcher

I faced in the big leagues. He took the mound with a simmering rage, throwing high-octane, angry stuff. Gibson didn't want you to hit a foul ball if he could help it. The season he had in 1968 was insane: in his 34 starts, there were 24 games where Gibson gave up one run or less. After starting the season 3–5, he went 12–0 in June and July, including a run in June of five straight complete game shutouts. Gibson went 10 innings once, 11 innings twice, and 12 innings during that season. The craziest numbers after seeing his season ERA of 1.12 is that Gibby lost nine games. How the hell can you pitch like he pitched for a team that went to the World Series and still lose nine games?

Bob Gibson's 1968 season was probably the biggest reason MLB voted to lower the height of the pitching mound from 15 to 10 inches, and to shrink the strike zone a tad to give us poor hitters a chance. But Gibson could have been pitching out of a foxhole and he still would have given me fits.

Shrinking the strike zone must have affected Gibson; his ERA for the 1969 season would nearly double from microscopic 1.12 to a merely phenomenal 2.18. It made no difference to us; we notched only three hits on the way to a 3–1 loss. Gaspar took a heavy 0-for-3 collar, and you could see the effect. This was the National League regular season, not spring training when pitchers are mostly just trying to throw strikes. And when the team ain't winning and you ain't hittin', you better hang loose. At 2–4, we had a wobble in our giddy-up out of the gate. We've just lost four straight, been swept in a three-game series by the reigning champion Cardinals, who were once again the team to beat in the early going. Joe Torre, who easily could have been a Met but who was instead grabbed by the Cards for Orlando Cepeda, dined out on our pitchers, going 5-for-11 against us with a couple of RBIs. The baseball season is long, but you can become an also-ran in a hurry.

Early Struggles

There would be no respite. We lost six out of eight. Gaspar was gasping, going one for his last 11. In Pittsburgh, he took an 0-for-4 in Gentry's second win, then an 0-for-4 against Bob Moose, then, in three times up in a loss against future U.S. senator Jim Bunning, a bunt single for Gaspar, which registered zero on Gil's Richter Scale. All managers can count, and Gaspar wasn't the only outfielder going bad. In that game, I hit for Tommie Agee, a player Gil had traded for the year before, but whose 0-for-3 put him officially in the weeds with a .195 BA. Agee had to cool it for a couple of games, watching the newbie Amos Otis patrol center field.

With Hodges, it wasn't personal. Nobody liked being benched, but as Gil told the *Daily News* about me the year before, "It's up to you." That applied to everyone. You knew what the deal was with Gil. You hit or you sit. It's the eternal catch-22. You need to play to build confidence, but if you don't produce, you don't play. It was as it should be, but it couldn't have been more frustrating for me. The team was struggling, Sham was still sidelined, and there were at bats available, if I could just do something. It was up to me, and I wasn't getting it done. . . .

Come April 19, Gaspar's 2-for-22 streak won me another start against . . . guess who? Bob Gibson. Oh Rodney, how can I thank you for that? Now, fifty years have passed, and if Gibson would walk into the room, I would get queasy. Predictably, I went 0-for-4 with three strikeouts, but Cleon and Krane drove in the runs that helped Seaver beat him 2–1. The next night, Nelson Briles had a tough time following Gibson's act, and we jumped him like a big, wet dog, getting 14 hits in an 11–3 win. I had a pair of knocks and three RBIs. Two in a row! But we couldn't keep the cold away.

We stumbled again, losing four out of five, including two losses at home in Shea to Ernie Banks, Billy Williams, Fergie Jenkins, and the rest of the Chicago Cubs, who had been hot, hot, hot. I had gone 4-for-10 with three RBIs, but we were dead last, six games back. During that mini-skid, Otis went quiet with a 1-for-17 run. The joke line back then was: You go that bad, you better get you a pair of pants with a double seat in them because your ass is going to be on the bench. It applied to all of us, including Tommie Agee, as Gaspar got another shot in center.

April ended with a mix of sunshine and showers. Jim McAndrew was on the mound for the series finale against the Cubs. Mac went five strong shutout innings but ripped open a blister on his pitching finger, a seemingly innocuous issue that would keep him out a month. Tug would come in with four clean innings and Cleon would win it with a walk-off, three-run bomb in the bottom of the ninth. Yeah, baby.

The month ended, and to no one's surprise we were a very mediocre 9–11. The big surprise was that the Cubs had rung up a sizzling 16–8. The bigger surprise was that the mighty Cardinals were 8–12, and staggering.

Warming Up

The loss of McAndrew was bad. The next night, things got worse. In Montreal, Koosman took the ball for us and cruised through 4.1 shutout innings. "I had an 0–2 count on [Expos catcher] John Bateman," recalls Koosman. "I threw an inside fastball, and my shoulder went numb."

There are only a couple of true warriors on any Major League Baseball team, guys who would fight alongside you, like Cleon, Tommie Agee, and Don Cardwell. Kooz was one of them. Nolan Ryan replaced Koosman, and with the help of his 4.2 shutout innings and two Kranepool solo homers, we won. Still, we spent the next two days in a funk. All we knew was that one of our foundation arms was hurting. Jerry flew back to New York to see Dr. Peter La-Motte, the team physician, who did a thorough exam and couldn't find anything wrong. Koosman then joined the team in Chicago and threw his regular bullpen session between starts. "I couldn't get the ball to home plate," recalled a frustrated Koosman,

Fortunately, our GM, Johnny Murphy, who had won 93 games during a thirteen-year major league career, had joined the team in Chicago. Johnny listened closely to the trainer, then said that it sounded like a problem he once had that turned out to be a knot in the muscle in his left armpit. Murphy then put his finger on Koosman's arm pit. "I damned near came off the table," Kooz said. "That's when Gus [Mauch] started milking that torn minor muscle and I cried for a month."

Try to figure this out. The Mets' record was 9–11. We would play seventeen games without Jerry Koosman on the mound. Somehow, we went a very decent ten and seven, which seemed almost miraculous. On May 5, we swept a doubleheader against the Cubs, a pair of 3–2 complete game wins by Seaver and McGraw. On May 6, our canny vet Don Cardwell went all-world against Cincinnati; not only does Cardy pitch a complete game, but he drives in three with one of four Met home runs, joining Cleon, Wayne Garrett, and Kenny Boswell. It's an 8–1 win and would mark the only time all season that we would hit four home runs. Go. Figure. We were a young team in search of an offensive identity, and this was not it.

On the 11th, we blew up the Astros' Don Wilson, who had no-hit the Big Red Machine his last time out. Wilson was a terrific pitcher who had won 104 games by the time he died in his prime at age twenty-nine in 1975. On May 21, we beat Atlanta 5–0 for our third win in a row. That lifted us to 18–18, the latest point in a season that any New York Mets team had a record as good as .500. A big part of the formula? Being smart enough to stand on the broad shoulders of Tom Seaver, who won five straight decisions, which is why we call him Tom Terrific. Now, .500 doesn't win you anything; we were still five and a half games behind the division-leading Cubs. But if we could make a charge without Koosman, what would happen when he got back?

I do have a lot of nerve using "we" so much in talking about this period. The correct response would have been, "What do you mean *we*, you got a hole in your pocket?" In fact, during most of this run, I had been next to useless. From April 30 on, I was immersed in a bone-numbing, confidence-cooking, 1-for-24 streak. You can't really know anything about hitting and have something like that happen to you. I was twenty-five years old, into my fifth year in the big leagues, seemingly on the verge of putting everything together and having the kind of season that would justify management's patience. Instead, it was a nightmare. I began to think that maybe they needed to lower the mound even more. The slump turned Hodges so far off me that I spent eight games sitting on the bench. I could have taken a cruise and not been missed. Sham was back in right field and hitting. Agee was back in center and swinging the bat good. Johnny Murphy had included me among his untouchables, but I felt like an untouchable in India. My shadow didn't reach the batter's box until a pinch-hit opportunity on May 22, a 15–3 drubbing by the Braves, most famous for being the game when Mike Lum hit a double pinch-hitting for Hank Aaron, the first time in 9,015 major league at bats that someone pinch hit for Hammering Hank. That started a five-game losing streak during which we fell from five to nine games back. We stunk worse than New York City during the 1968 garbage strike.

It was maddening. You're working hard every day, trying to put something back together, all the while your stock is sinking lower than whale poop. Honestly, if either Rod Gaspar or Amos Otis had gotten hot, I could have found myself in the minors. But they struggled, too. Not that it made me feel any better.

Hitting was supposed to be my meal ticket, but my play in the outfield annoyed me, and Gasper's presence proved that the team execs would not forever be immune to the attractions of a more rounded player. In the starts I got, if the game was at all close, Hodges usually replaced me late with Gaspar, the better defender. It drove me crazy, ate at me, but I was hardly unusual among Met outfielders. I needed more work.

In pregame practice, outfielders handled two ground balls, throwing to second base, fielded two more grounders throwing to third, and two more throwing home. Then we collected in deep right or left and someone, usually a pitcher, hit big, stupid fly balls that did little to improve our fielding. Shagging flies hit by a fungo is about as pleasant an activity as there is in baseball. It was so relaxing. While you're drifting under big, lazy fly balls, you can check the wind and see how the sun affects your position, but they won't make you better.

Eddie Yost—Yostie—showed up in 1968 as Gil Hodges's third base coach, and boy could he handle a fungo. He'd played eighteen years, mostly at third for the Senators in the 1940s and 1950s, leading the American League in bases on balls six times, earning the nickname The Walking Man. He held the record for lifetime lead-off homers, 29, until Barry Bonds broke it.

I asked Yostie to get me on the angry end of his fungo bat. He had patience and a master's degree in physical education from NYU. I worked him hard, I worked me hard. These were intense fifteen-minute sessions before games. I wore the man out. I grinded him to where he didn't want to see me coming. He drilled me with line drives and ground balls from about 150 feet. The point: do the exercise at game speed, and read the ball off the bat quickly, almost instantaneously. I figured if I read them better, the little popups would get easier, and I could put the routine back into routine fly balls. It turned out I was right. My glove and my footwork for releasing throws got better. My whole diagnosis of a fly ball improved. Eventually, Hodges stopped removing me for defense. It would have been a total victory if I'd tried to learn as much about hitting. I surely would have played a few more years.

In the real world, my favorite diversion was anything about our space program, and fortunately for me, it was in high gear. Apollo 10, the full dress rehearsal for the scheduled lunar landing, had taken off and was sending the first color photos of earth back our way. Apollo 10, with its crew of Thomas Stafford, Eugene Cernan, and John Young, did everything but land on the moon. The cost for pushing the red go button to launch the Saturn V booster was a little over a billion dollars in current money but that booster, only developed because of the genius of Wernher von Braun, our favorite former Nazi rocket scientist, never failed. Although recent communications transcripts released from Apollo 10 give light to a more human situation that had to be handled. It was truly a "Houston, we have a potty problem" moment. In their usual unperturbed manner, it was Stafford who said, "Give me a napkin quick. There's a turd floating through the air." All of this followed by laughter and questions of, "Who did it?" The answer was never revealed but with a three-man crew, it couldn't have been too hard for them to figure out.

The Streak

Just as quickly as we reached the heights of mediocrity, we tumbled back down, losing five straight, including three in a row to the Astros, the only team that we would finish 1969 with a losing record against. Still, no one panicked, least of all Hodges. Having survived Okinawa no doubt gave him perspective on how to handle setbacks, especially in a kids game.

There was a wonderfully graphic story some old guys told us about Bobby Bragan, the manager of the then Milwaukee Braves in the early 1960s. The team was beyond losing—they were playing like horseshit—to the point where Bragan turned on them. With everybody sitting at their lockers, as the story goes, Bragan said, "Some of you guys are fucking me. Well, fuck me? No—*fuck you.*" He then went down the row, pointing his finger at each man. "Fuck you, fuck you, and fuck you!" Whereupon, Eddie Mathews, his All-Star third baseman and the author of 512 home runs during his seventeen-year career, interrupted, "Fuck me, Bobby?"

"No, not you, Eddie!" Bragan corrected himself. "But fuck the rest of you guys!"

Well, nothing like that was ever going to happen to us, that just wasn't Gil's style. His style, in fact, was to say as little as possible. Which was a good thing because something started that nobody could have predicted. After it happened, I believe Hodges and the Mets organization looked at us in a whole different light.

You don't usually start a winning streak by not scoring a run in the first nine innings of the first game of the string, but then, why not? As long as you don't give up any. And that's where Jerry Koosman came in. Koosman was back. The magic fingers of Gus Mauch had massaged away the painful knot under Kooz's left arm. "I couldn't believe how good it felt." We couldn't believe how well he pitched.

On May 28, Kooz gave us 10 shutout innings against San Diego. They left the bases loaded in the second inning, and nothing much from anyone happened until the bottom of the 11th, after Cleon, me, and Buddy Harrelson managed to link three singles, the last a walk-off base hit. One–zip Mets. It was Ken Boswell's last game before his two-week stretch of active duty in the Army Reserve started.

Next on the schedule, the West Coast came to town: three games each against the San Francisco Giants and the Los Angeles Dodgers. I always loved playing those two teams. In my rookie year the Giants were Mays, McCovey, and Marichal, and the Dodgers were Koufax and Drysdale. Everything about the Mets' look is an amalgamation of the Dodgers and the Giants. Our orange is from the Giants, as is the block lettering of the NY on our hats; from the Dodgers we took the royal blue and the scripted Mets signature on our home unis.

Game one dispelled the warm and fuzzies as Tom Seaver found himself in the bottom of the seventh down 3–nothing. That's when I led off with a solo bomb against the well-traveled lefty Mike McCormick. We scored three more in the bottom of the eighth. Gaspar went deep leading off, I singled in another run, and catcher Duffy Dyer drove home the go-ahead run for a 4–3 victory. The next night, in front of more than thirty thousand fans, we faced Hall of Famer Gaylord Perry, always a chore. San Fran took a 2–0 lead, which our veteran third baseman, Ed Charles, "The Glider," erased with a three-run blow after two were out in the bottom of the fourth. The moment gave birth to a mantra: Never throw a slider to the Glider. Gary Gentry was solid for the 4–2 win. On the next day, in front of 41,000 spending a Sunday at Shea, we had another comeback win and a sweep. Your boy would single in a run early, and then, tied at four with the bases loaded in the ninth, I executed the rare walk-off WALK! As in, ball four, we win. 5–4 Mets. It was the 1st of June, and if you were one of those cup-is-half-full people, you're pretty happy that we've won four straight. If you're a half-empty type, you see that we're a game below .500, in third place, nine games back of a Chicago team that is playing at a sizzling .667 pace.

We took the first two games from the Dodgers with a gem by Koosman and another win by Seaver. On Wednesday, June 4, in front of 31,000, we started Jack DiLauro in the series capper. Jack pitched only 63.2 innings for the Mets all year, but he threw nine of them that day, and they were prime, completely shutting L.A. out. Too bad for him that we weren't hitting any better. The game went scoreless into the top of the 15th, with the Dodgers going 0-for-14 with runners in scoring position. Hard to do. Finally, with one out and Tommie Agee on first, Wayne Garrett singled and center fielder Willie Davis let the ball get by him, allowing Agee to come all the way home. It would be one of only six errors Willie would make on the season, the only Dodger miscue of the night, and it cost them big-time. In what had become a seven-game win streak, we had won five games by one run, while scoring a puny thirteen runs. The math is easy. That's a little less than two runs a game. More accurately, that is a lot of great pitching. Fate was loving us. We hopped a flight for the West Coast. Jet lag be damned, the Padres were waiting for us in San Diego.

The next night, we were tied at three, bottom of the eighth. Cleon singled and stole second with two outs. He was the go-ahead run in scoring position, and I was up. I was 0–2 with a walk, and I'm getting ready to step in when Hodges calls me back from the on-deck circle and sends up Shamsky to pinch hit against the righty Gary Ross.

Later in my career, with the Yankees in 1971, in a game against the Tigers, Ralph Houk had me starting in the cleanup spot against the veteran righty Dean Chance, once the Cy Young Award winner, then in his last season of baseball. In the top of the first inning we load the bases with nobody out, and I'm walking up to hit. I can't imagine why somebody's trying to get my attention. It's Houk, and he wants to send up Ron Blomberg, a left-hander, the man destined to become the game's first designated hitter, to pinch hit. That hook blindsided me.

I can't say that Gil's decision hit me the same way. Coming into that at bat in San Diego in '69, I'd fallen into a streak of my own, as in, 0 for my last 15. Sure, I wanted to hit, but if I was really surprised, then shame on me. What was surprising was what the Padres did. Shamsky had been swinging the bat well; with first base open and our catcher, Jerry Grote, a right-handed hitter who was batting .230 on the year and hitless on the night, due next, the smart play was to walk Shamsky and pitch to Grote. Instead, the Padres pitched to Shamsky. Bad idea. He drove in Cleon with a single, and we had our eighth in a row.

Number nine came the next night, facing the old Dodger hero, Johnny Podres. Podres pitching for the Padres? It's a baseball line that just dances, although not as much as his off-speed stuff. We got men on, but we squandered a lot of chances, managing to amass a mere 1–0 lead in the seventh. But with two outs, I tripled in Cleon, and the Glider picked me up with a double. Koosman cruised the rest of the way and we sealed the deal 3–1. At this point you don't need a clubhouse speech by the manager to tell you that something special is in the air. Now you feel like you're playing with house money.

Sham's in the lineup against the Padres' right-hander Al Santorini. By now, comebacks have become commonplace. Down 2–zip? No problem. Agee, Garrett, and the Krane drove in the runs, one in the seventh, two in the eighth. Seaver was money through nine, 3–2 Mets. And then there were ten. I've never been in this place before. No complacency in the clubhouse, just a confident, even keel, carrying us up the coast to San Francisco to face Mike McCormick. The wise old man of our pitching staff, Don Cardwell, spots the Giants a run, but he's pitching great. In the top of the fourth, Agee bombs one and we're tied. In the fifth, the twelve-year vet Cardwell sac-flies the go ahead, and finally Cleon launches a three-run bolt. We roll 'em 9–4.

But then it dawns on me. We've won eleven straight. We're 29–23, six games over .500, with a firm hold on second place, safely ahead of the Cardinals, who are dangerous but who can't seem to stop digging themselves into a hole. On the other hand, we're still seven games back of the Chicago Cubs, who have won eleven out of thirteen and are 37–17, twenty full games over .500 with a third of the season not yet over. That realization left me with a feeling in my gut like I'd get after a perfectly wonderful night of drinking. After so many years of frustration and losing, here were my New York Mets making serious strides into respectability, and attaining a level of success no Mets team had ever experienced. Yet, thanks to Leo Durocher and the Chicago Cubs, we might had ended up as the pumpkin in somebody else's Cinderella story.

The Trade

What we didn't know was that similar thoughts were bubbling around the front office. Right on the June 15 trading deadline, our GM, Johnny Murphy, announced what amounted to a five-for-one trade with the Montreal Expos. The most talented player the Expos received was Steve Renko, a young right-handed pitcher who would validate the deal with his fifteen years in the big leagues, including eight mostly productive seasons in Montreal. The other fellows did not leave a big mark. We, in return, received Donn Clendenon, a reliable major league hitter.

Eight years a Pittsburgh Pirate before getting moved up north, Donn was well-known as one of those talkative specimens, a self-appointed authority on the game of baseball and life. In 1969, when baseball put too much traveling music on him, Clendenon put on the brakes. It started when the Pirates left him exposed in the expansion draft in the off-season of 1968. Clink, as everyone called him, became an Expo with the brand-new team in Montreal. Clink wasn't all that hot to play north of the border, but when the Expos tried to deal him to the Houston Astros for Rusty Staub, Donn had no desire to go to Texas and play for Harry "The Hat" Walker, who was regarded as a dyed-in-the-wool racist. Donn had seen enough of that with Harry in Pittsburgh. He made it clear that he would rather go lawyer for the Scripto Pen Company, and declared himself a holdout.

There were other issues in Donn's world; his Dad was sick and would pass away before the end of the season. The issue fell in the lap of new MLB commissioner Bowie Kuhn, whose grand compromise was to have Clendenon agree to end his holdout, get in shape, and play for Montreal, while the team worked on a trade to somewhere he wanted to play. When the New York Mets offered their list of four players, the Expos said yes, and Donn said, "Most definitely," and changed his area code to the Big Apple.

Clendenon's arrival at the end of June was a huge dose of adrenaline to a Mets team that had shown its bona fides with our eleven-game win streak. We were thrilled that we had acquired a masher of his stature without yielding any of our high-ceiling young arms or any of the so-called untouchable position players. Donn came in the door knowing what we all knew: we had the arms to win, but we needed to score more runs, and he had been recruited to be the difference maker. "The Mets needed somebody to pound the ball," Clendenon told *The New York Times*'s Leonard Koppett. "That was my job." Clendenon changed our offense not only by what he could do, but what he helped others do. By getting on base, and by posing a threat that pitchers tried to avoid, he made sure that the hitters behind him would start getting better pitches to hit. Down the stretch, as Clendenon got rolling, I benefited from that as much as anyone.

What we didn't know was if he would ever shut up. Clink was a nonstop talker. "I kept the team loose. I got on everybody, black and white." He was an equal-opportunity ragger. From Tom Seaver to

Rod Gaspar, it didn't matter to him, he'd be in your shit all the time but in a way that kept everybody loose and together. He'd call Gaspar, a backup outfielder, PeePee for his lack of pop at the plate. He dubbed Jim McAndrew, a right-handed pitcher with a baby face and big-boy stuff, Moms, because McAndrew would sometimes look like he wanted his Mommy to come visit him on the mound. He pulled it off with an intellectual and athletic authority that seemed completely engaged and yet a little above it all. If he wasn't so smart and such a good hitter, he couldn't have gotten away with it. Clendenon had the skins on the wall, as a productive veteran of many campaigns. He was larger than life. He had swagger. He was just what we needed.

Later in life, when we were all done with the game, Clendenon was diagnosed with a form of leukemia. It was of a type that doctors could, with treatment, hold at bay, but never cure. Donn passed away in September 2005, in Sioux Falls, South Dakota, where he lived and practiced law. He was seventy years old. The Mets had a memorial for him at Shea Stadium. I came up from Baltimore, where I was staying with my Mom, who was in the late stages of the cancer that would take her life. My home in New Orleans was struggling back from the ravages of Hurricane Katrina. As part of our remembrances, Ed Charles, our veteran third baseman, was reading a poem dedicated to Donn that he had written, when my phone started ringing so I stepped out into the hallway. It was a friend of mine in New Orleans, telling me that the electricity was back on for the first time in a month. It meant that Cecilia and I could go home.

Summer in the City

The Clendenon trade had such a large and immediate impact on our team that I was surprised to look back and see that his debut for the Mets came a full four days after his acquisition. Assigned to be the right-handed part of our first base platoon (matching Ed Kranepool), Donn entered the last game of a four-game set with Philly in the ninth inning as a pinch runner for J.C. Martin, our backup catcher. With nobody out, I hit for Al Weis, and I scratched a single off Al Raffo, a six foot five righty who was playing in his only season in the bigs. Jerry Grote pinch hit for the pitcher, Ron Taylor, and bunted us over to second and third, when Ken Boswell singled to left and both Clendenon and I scored. 6–5 Mets, and McGraw saved it.

That stirring comeback win came in front of 6,000 less-than-impressed fans in Philly. The next night, June 20, back in New York, where there is always a lot to do, no doubt some number of our fans decided to do something else. Maybe catch *Oh! Calcutta!*, an all-nude musical that had opened Off-Broadway to outraged and sellout crowds. Some were no doubt toasting Congressman Adam Clayton Powell, the controversial spokesman on civil rights matters, who had just won a significant case before the Supreme Court. And later in June, some were rioting at the Stonewall Inn, a gay bar in Greenwich Village, a time of anger and protest that inaugurated the gay rights movement in the United States.

But out in Queens, 54,000 of our fans showed up at Shea Stadium to watch the Mets take on Bob Gibson and the St. Louis Cardinals. One of them was Vladimir Horowitz, the brilliant classical pianist and composer. Before the game, Vladimir, a Russian émigré, visited our clubhouse, and Gil Hodges invited me to say hello. Mr. Horowitz was born in Kiev, Ukraine, and told me that "svoboda" meant freedom in Ukrainian, which in fact I knew; in those days in New York, there was a newsstand in almost every corner and on every subway platform, which displayed newspapers in about thirty languages; one of them was a Ukrainian daily newspaper published in New York under the banner, "Svoboda." I would be lying if I said I knew very much about Mr. Horowitz; in those days, you couldn't just call up his Wikipedia page and listen to his incredible performances on YouTube, which you absolutely should do. This man was one of the greatest talents ever to sit down at a piano, breathing life into scores by Chopin, Bach, Rachmaninoff, and so many others. The maestro was sixty-six years old when we met. We admired each other's hands and shook as he was leaving our clubhouse. I learned later that he was actually a Cardinal fan, and I wondered if he was aware what happened to me against his Cardinals that Sunday.

Bob Gibson got the ball in the series opener and I wasn't too bothered that my name was not in the lineup. Thankfully, Cleon Jones felt more secure. He was hitting .340 for the season, and wasted no time, touching up Gibby for a two-run blow in the first, Art Shamsky added a sac fly for three quick ones, and the Mets would hold on 4–3. After a loss on Saturday, Clendenon got his first start at first base in the first game of a Sunday doubleheader. Most people under the age of sixty don't remember doubleheaders, but for many years they were regularly scheduled on summer Sundays. They were good for fans, in that you were almost certain to see all the fellows on your squad, and they were good for players, since the usual result was a complete day off during most weeks, which I believe was a good thing for your mental state. As players earned more money, owners wanted more individual gates, so scheduled doubleheaders started disappearing. By the 1980s they were virtually gone.

In game one of that Sunday double dip against the Cards, the Mets battered Steve Carlton, although somebody must have misplaced my invitation to the party. Carlton K'ed me my first two times up. No big deal, but the whiffs didn't stop there. Turns out your boy was working his way into a legendary professional nightmare. The Mets knocked Carlton out in the bottom of the fourth, but while Steve could take a shower and start putting the bad day behind him, I continued to construct the ugliest 0-for-5 you can imagine. After Carlton got me twice, it was Chuck Taylor's turn. Taylor was a decent major league right-hander, who pitched parts of eight seasons in the show. He made it three straight Ks. Then in came Ron Willis, another decent righty for the Cards who would tragically succumb to a brain tumor at the age of thirty-four. He rang me up twice—the second time, to add insult to injury, when he intentionally walked Clink to load the bases to pitch to me. Why wouldn't he? I couldn't object to the strategy. I had already K'ed four times. When I fouled one off early in the count, I can remember hearing a smattering of sarcastic applause. They might have been rooting for a K, if only to say they had witnessed something historic, if historically bad. With my last swing and a miss, I became only the thirteenth player in major league history to strike out five times. After the game, a reporter asked if I heard the fans booing. . . . "When you strike out five times in a game," I said, "they should line up and boo you all the way home!" (Some visual, huh?)

For me, I was feeling frustration on an epic level. You have a bat in your hand, there's a baseball being thrown through the strike zone, but for an entire afternoon getting the former to intersect with the latter on a common plane just wouldn't happen. "They booed and they booed," Wayne Garrett, our young infielder, recalled. "I was thinking, how can they boo one of us?" I heard it, too. Here I am, in my mid-twenties, at what should be the intellectual and physical peak of my professional ability, and this happens. It's like the "it" you've heard about for pitchers when they forget how to throw strikes. Unlike Cleon, I didn't understand the mechanics of hitting. I was a "feel" guy all the way. When I felt it, I could hit it. Now, all I felt was doubt and nausea. This had never happened to me at any level of amateur or professional baseball. Five awful strikeouts, where you were never in any of the at bats. My gut wrenched, like I was falling through my own asshole. At the nexus between urgency and fear, I felt like a big dump would make everything better, except I was afraid what might come out would be my heart. Looking back over all this time, five straight strikeouts in front of 55,000 people felt like walking out onstage, bare-assed naked, in *Oh! Calcutta!*, and forgetting all your lines. I may have actually had that dream.

The year before, against the Houston Astros in the Astrodome, in a 23-inning game we would lose 1–0, I went 0-for-10, with five fly outs and five strikeouts. That was bad, but this was a higher level of bad. I tried some humor afterward, as forced as it was, saying, "Sure I was eating my heart out, but because we won the game, I'm only eating one ventricle." Some writers thought that was funny; to me it felt lame. I was freaking destroyed. I remember saying that occasionally in my big league career, I felt like the guy running with his suitcases trying to catch a train pulling out of the station while the stars, like Seaver, Koosman, and Clendenon, were sitting in the bar car sipping drinks. Five straight Ks felt like getting run over by the train.

While I went colder than whale shit in the Atlantic, the Cubs stayed hot. (No more references to whale dung—I promise.) From May 28 to June 24, the Mets went on a torrid 20–5 run. That's us playing .800 ball through a 25-game stretch and hardly closing the gap on Chicago. Really ridiculous. In the second half of that run, we won seven of eight games, including two back-to-back complete game gems by Koosman and Seaver, capped by an eight-inning jewel by Jim McAndrew. The net improvement for us versus the Cubs in the standings was a game and a half. In that 25-game period, the Cubs won two out of three and still led us by five, so there were no cracks appearing in the Cubs armor.

Instead, they accumulated milestones. Billy Williams eclipsed Stan Musial's National League record, playing in 896 games in a row. Billy was thirty-one years old and Ernie Banks, Mr. Cub, the soul of the team, a guy I had gone with on my second USO tour to Vietnam, was thirty-eight. Despite their age, they played every day, as did Ron Santo, their All-Star third baseman, and Don Kessinger, the Cubs' steady shortstop. Soon Old Man Time would present his bill for all their dedication. The Mets were younger, better rested, had a deeper pitching staff, used a five-man starting rotation instead of four starters, and had just acquired Donn Clendenon to make us stronger. But while Chicago had an older lineup and worked from a four-man rotation with fewer options out of the bullpen, nobody was sitting around waiting for them to stumble. They were still setting the pace, holding first place.

The megalopolis of New York was always great at making you aware that more than just your stuff was happening. You might think we would have owned the sports pages, but there were rumblings from the NFL. After winning the Super Bowl in January, Joe Namath's playboy image, which we all envied, had grown only larger. Now came the news that Joe and a couple of buddies had opened a bar in Manhattan, Bachelors III. Instantly it became the hottest place in town, drawing celebrities from the show business and sports worlds (including Art Shamsky and Ken Boswell and other Mets who lived in Manhattan), but also a few too many gamblers and mafia types. NFL Commissioner Pete Rozelle ordered— you heard that right, *ordered*—Joe Willie to divest himself. At first, Namath dug in his heels and threatened to retire. And why not? He was only twenty-six years old, and lived in a Midtown apartment that featured a giant white long-haired llama skin rug that someone could get lost in. Having once visited that apartment, I am confident that perhaps more than one young, big-city lady actually did. It took only a couple of days before Joe's mega-celebrity gave way to good sense, and he got out of the bar business.

We were solidly in the midst of a 20–5 streak, and when the Phillies limped into town 12 games under .500, we started to think the schedule never looked more propitious. Maybe the Phils did, too; they were playing without veteran stars Johnny Callison and Deron Johnson and their young-and-coming shortstop Don Money, and in the first two games of the series at Shea they went belly-up. They were also without the best hitter on the team, first baseman Richie Allen, a name to which he answered grudgingly. But his absence was unexpected.

Like the rest of his teammates, Allen was scheduled to show up at Shea for a doubleheader on Tuesday, June 24. But first he drove to Monmouth Park, New Jersey, to visit his thoroughbred, Trick Fire. Monmouth Park is about seventy miles from Shea Stadium, but that's seventy miles full of rivers and people and trucks with flat tires and other obstacles to human progress. Either oblivious or not terribly concerned, Allen missed the afternoon start time for the double dip. When at last he began heading for the stadium, he learned via the Phillies' radio broadcast that his manager, Bob Skinner, the former major league left fielder/first baseman, who had been hired midseason 1968 and who would be fired midseason 1969, had announced that Allen had been suspended indefinitely. Whereupon Richie sensibly enough turned his vehicle around and headed back to Philadelphia.

For Phillies fans and management, the blush was off the rose for Richie, not yet Dick, and he was making all the noises of a man who wanted out. Saying once that, "God didn't bless me with the gift of words," what words he blessed the fans with were scratched in large capital letters with his spikes in the dirt around first base. When they booed him, Allen scratched out, "BOO." I don't know if Phillies fans invented booing, but they certainly refined it into an art form. Another time Allen wrote, "OCT 2," the last day of the season, surely suggesting that he was anxious to reach that date. When Commissioner Bowie Kuhn suggested that Allen cease his infield messaging, he wrote, "WHY." He would have loved Twitter.

Back before helmets were required to feature earflaps in the early 1970s and more recently, optional face guards, they didn't. (*Photo by Co Rentmeester/The LIFE Premium Collection/Getty Images*)

Yours truly, trying to act like he belonged between two Giants' Hall of Famers Willie Mays and the late Willie McCovey. (*Photo by Kidwiler Collection/Diamond Images/Getty Images*)

Down the home stretch in 1969, I was half of the right field platoon with Art Shamsky. Cleon Jones was our left fielder, and Tommie Agee played center. (*Photo by Frank Hurley/New York* Daily News *Archive/Getty Images*)

It always seemed to me that as Casey Stengel traveled between the clubhouse and the playing field during any Mets Oldtimer's Day, he grew younger. (*Bettman/Getty Images*)

What this memoir should make clear with even casual reading is that Gil Hodges had one of the most adroit baseball minds you will ever encounter. A relationship that I failed to appreciate when it really mattered. (*Bruce Bennett*)

I wanted to play all of right field, including every inch of the wall behind me. (*Photo by William N. Jacobellis/*New York Post *Archives/©NYP Holdings, Inc./Getty Images*)

Met fans tried to will me good luck with charms, which I hung off my name tag in recognition. (*Photo by Frank Hurley/New York* Daily News *Archive/Getty Images*)

It's never too soon to celebrate. Here I am with J. C. Martin, Tom Seaver, and Donn Clendenon after wc beat the O's 2–1 in Game 4 to take a 3–1 series lead. (*Photo by B Bennett/Bruce Bennett Studios/Getty Images*)

After our World Series win in 1969, a lot of us smelled like shaving cream for a week or so! (*Photo by John Duprey/New York* Daily News *Archive/Getty Images*)

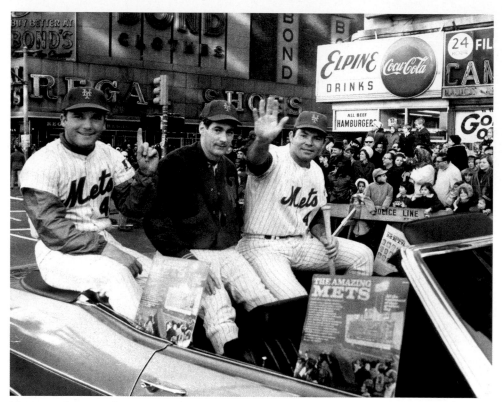

This was the Macy's Day Parade in 1969, as your boy sat to the left of our two Mets closers, Dr. Ron Taylor and Tug McGraw. (*Photo by Hal Mathewson/New York* Daily News *Archive/Getty Images*)

For a full year I worked at drawing, a little bit every day. It culminated with this pencil drawing of my World Series glove. And, really, ended with it too. (*Photo courtesy of the author*)

Not having to manage him in the big leagues, I loved Richie Allen. He swung 38 ounces like a man and hit balls where nobody lived. But he did dance to his own music. In my first couple of years playing in old Connie Mack Stadium, I remember getting on first base when he was playing there, and he'd have liquor on his breath while his eyes looked like two piss holes in the snow. What was unbelievable was how well he played smelling like he just crawled out of a glass of Scotch. In my rookie year I had a play with him one time at third base. I got too far down the line and a pickoff throw came from the catcher. I thought I was out and started walking away. Allen had dropped the ball when he tagged me, picked it up, and tagged me again. I was sure I was out this time but he dropped the ball again and this time when I walked away, Allen tagged me for the third time and that did it. In baseball, you get three outs in an inning. That's the only time in my career that I got all of mine on one play at one base.

So, we would miss Richie Allen (he would return as a somewhat happier Dick Allen, and have some prodigious seasons for the White Sox and one with the Cardinals), but we enjoyed seeing the Phillies with their star AWOL and other injured regulars. After sweeping the doubleheader, we felt pretty confident sending Nolan Ryan against Lowell Palmer, a bit of a character who wore dark shades even for night games. He said his eyes were sensitive to light. Although he was en route to a 2–8 season, he was a sidearm pitcher with a hard sinker/slider that could be very nasty.

Behind Palmer was a less than scary lineup. Larry Hisle, a twenty-two-year-old outfielder, led off. He had some pop and could steal a base, but he was just in the second of his starry fourteen big league seasons, and was not yet the dangerous hitter he would become. In the two hole was Cookie Rojas, who at thirty was off to a good start, with good years left in his sixteenth major league season. But after losing two, manager Skinner juggled the lineup. He put

Dave Watkins, primarily a catcher, at third base, the only game at that position in the only year he ever played in the big leagues, and moved Rick Joseph, a Dominican infielder from San Pedro de Macorís who would sadly lose his life to diabetes at age forty, to second base. Johnny Briggs was a pretty good hitting outfielder, but he was off to a terrible start, batting .155 here in late June. Briggs hit behind Watkins with Joseph in the four hole. In the five spot was 1B Gene Stone, less than 30 ABs in the big leagues, all of them in 1969. Behind him, batting sixth, Mike Ryan, a light-hitting catcher, followed by Ron Stone, no relation to Gene, about four seasons up, was hitting .178, and eighth, at short was Terry Harmon, a good-field, no-hit utility infielder.

There's a term in baseball, "he was just a guy," not meant as a rip but to describe a marginal talent, way short of an impact player. I considered myself "just a guy" and proud of it. So, here are the Mets at home and as hot as we have been all season and, really, in our history at that point, and if there was a major league lineup you wanted to face, what Philly ran out there that day was it. And after five innings, what we expected was coming true: we were ahead 5–zip, Nolan Ryan was throwing little aspirin tablets, and I'm planted on my padded seat in the dugout, leaning back, thinking for the first time in my career that we were the Harlem Globetrotters playing the Washington Generals. I mean, the thought crept into my head like an earworm you can't get rid of: these poor bastards don't have a chance. Or so I thought.

Things went sour two ways: first gradually, then suddenly. We stopped hitting. After five innings, we made nothing but outs, the kind of thing that happens so quietly that you hardly realize it's happening until the game is all but over. At first there's no cause for alarm; Ryan is pitching in the top of the seventh with a 5–1 lead. Then Philly nursed a walk and hit a single, at which point an error by our third baseman lets one in. Then Ryan threw a wild pitch, and then Ron Stone hit a single, and now the lead has been cut to one. Which would have been plenty, except in the eighth, Dave Watkins took Cal Koonce deep for one of his four major league homers, all of them in 1969 and we were tied, and tumbling into extra innings. But not for long. In the 10th, Dave Watkins returned to the plate and whacked a triple, the only triple he would ever hit in the big leagues, and then scored on a single by Johnny Briggs. I was stunned; I had been sitting there, dumb and happy in the dugout, awash in sympathy until we choked on it. And if I was stunned then, I became utterly astonished over the next couple weeks as this bunch of "just guys" ran up a nine-game win streak. That taught me something I never again forgot: any man good enough to put on a big league uniform can kick you right in the ass. Even this bunch of Phillies, who would eventually lose 99 games.

I remember talking about this game with the Phils' radio broadcaster, the late Richie Ashburn. A Hall of Famer and twice the batting champion of the National League, Richie was still an expert on horseshit baseball, having played on the 1962 New York Mets who lost 120 games, still the gold standard for MLB ineptitude. He loved to tell stories from back then, like when Stengel spoke to the team at the end of that dismal first season. "Boys," he said, "you're probably gonna catch a lot of hell from the press for losing 120 games. But I don't want anybody here to take it personally. I want you all to remember that it was a team effort. Good luck."

All I know is that my first thought after that game was written all in caps, like Richie Allen had scratched it into my brain. SWOBODA, DON'T YOU EVER, EVER, EVER FEEL ANYTHING RESEMBLING PITY FOR ANY TEAM YOU'RE PLAYING IN THE MIDDLE OF AN UNDECIDED BIG LEAGUE GAME. That is right up there with premature celebration, and perhaps, premature ejaculation, as one of the worst things you can do. In its unique and unforgiving nature, retribution wrought by the gods of baseball is reserved for those who think they have anything "in the bag" before the final out. Or as the immortal Yogi Berra said, with a good deal more economy, "It ain't over till it's over."

Shoot the Moon

Falling through the bottom of June and into July, we rolled through a reasonably ugly string, losing six of eight games, including the first two July games in St. Louis. We were still in second place behind the Cubs, but now we trailed by eight games, and we needed all the patience and steadiness that the veterans like Ed Charles provided. In an occupation where every pitch, every at bat, every game can have decisive consequences, it was important for us young guys to sit around with Ed and listen to him talk about the rocky road he traveled through his sixteen years in the pros. We called him "The Glider" for the graceful way he moved around third base, for the soft throws to first base that seemed to glide and also for the graceful way he carried himself in this life.

One of the bedrock beauties of baseball is that an out can be infinity. Baseball is timeless, and every once in a while, without warning, it proves it to you. On July 2, our co-ace, Jerry Koosman, was fashioning a masterpiece, shutting out the Cardinals 4–0. Wayne Garrett had driven in three of the four runs. Then, with two quick outs in the bottom of the eighth, Koosman walked the bags full and Hodges lifted him for reliever Ron Taylor. The Cardinals sent lefty Vic Davalillo up to hit for Julian Javier, which brought us full-faced with another beautiful thing about baseball. It is a game of moments and like the Phils proved, as long as you have a big league uniform on, given an opportunity, you can become the man of that moment. Davalillo, smallish at five foot seven and 155 pounds, was the eighth Venezuelan to play in the majors. His game was speed and contact, but on that night he played Popeye and launched a grand slam home run, one of only two home runs by him that season, producing four of his season's 10 RBIs, and tying the game at four. One pattern that had emerged was that we might get beaten in a ball game, but it was rare when we gave up a lead late in a game. It was shocking to see Taylor blow his third save of the year, and to give way to Tug McGraw, who was about to have the definitive outing of his season.

McGraw, who had joined the Marine Reserves a couple of years back, had spent the off-season at boot camp and serving six months' active duty. He returned a different guy. Just as much fun, maybe more, but with a confidence and resolve that was hard to rattle. His line on the score sheet that day says it all. McGraw, in six innings of work, was touched for seven hits and walked four, but he stranded eleven Cardinals and gave up NO RUNS. Twice the winning run for the Cards was thrown out at home plate. It was an escape that Harry Houdini would have envied. Our GM, Johnny Murphy, a pretty decent relief pitcher himself, felt that this game was a watershed for Tug, or so he told Leonard Koppett. "After that game, I think, he never lacked confidence that he could get through any situation." It did seem that as Tug moved into his relief career, he didn't pitch his best until he got a couple of guys on base. And then he could really pitch. Just like in this Cardinals game that we should have won easily, then we should have lost easily . . . and then, on Ken Boswell's single, we won it in 14 innings.

By every force that holds the universe in balance, the Cards should have lost this game in regulation, but they tied it. Faced with so many opportunities in extra innings, they should have won it. But no. Games have a shape to them, and this one was surreal. It might surprise you to know that Salvador Dali, one of the great Surrealist painters, admired American baseball and he would have loved this one. I am reminded because on a shelf in my office I have a Dali-decorated baseball from his museum in St. Petersburg, Florida. The baseball came from my friend John Stinson, without whom this memoir would not exist. I was originally introduced to the museum after my baseball life by, yes, Tug McGraw. We were in St. Pete, where the Mets held spring training for so many years, invited by the Tampa Bay Rays for an Old Timers' celebration that included Tom Seaver and Donn Clendenon in early 2000. Tug, showing another surprising facet of himself, walked me over to the Dali Museum, and we both left with large catalogue books of Dali's complete works. I don't recall Tug and I making the Dali-baseball connection at the time, but the quote from the master himself goes, "About the game, I know nothing. But as an artist, I am obsessed." I think Dali saw baseball as ballet. The animated short film *Destino,* conceived by Dali and Walt Disney in 1946 and completed as a very different work in 2003 by Roy Disney, Walt's son, makes the point. There is a completely incongruous transition in the fanciful dance of love between a man and a woman, where he turns into a baseball player and she becomes a ballerina, sending a baseball his way, which he connects with in a beautiful, left-handed swing. I recommend that you google *Destino* and see it for yourself.

On Friday of the July 4th weekend, 1969, something borrowing another Spanish word but, more terrible and real came ashore off Lake Erie: the Fireworks Derecho. Meaning "straight" in Spanish, derecho is a meteorological term for a huge phalanx of thunderstorms. In this case, the phalanx was some two hundred miles long. The storms rumbled off the lake with 100 mph winds, spawning tornados with supersized hail. The storms rolled toward Cleveland, where folks in small pleasure boats had collected offshore to watch the scheduled July 4th fireworks display. Instead they saw the sky take on a shade of green, before unleashing storms that dealt death and destruction. Hundreds of boats were capsized, trees were uprooted, houses damaged, and eighteen people died in

Ohio alone, as this monster storm caught everybody in its path in the wrong place at the wrong time.

We were in Pittsburgh, taking on the Pirates, sweeping them in a doubleheader on the 4th. The remnants of this deadly derecho made it our way and rained us out Saturday night. On Sunday, I got my butt off the bench where it seemed glued thanks to my lack of performance. They don't make bats long enough to get base hits from the dugout, but Hodges, like any manager, was looking for a hot hand, and it hadn't been me for quite a while. Opportunities would present themselves, unannounced, along the way, coming off the bench for Cleon or Tommie Agee, as it did in Pittsburgh on July 6 after the second inning with the Mets down 6–1. Might have looked like a good time to rest your center fielder knowing that a significant series with the Cubs was coming next in New York. The bonus for me was that I came in for Agee, got a couple of hits, drove in a run, and scored when Clendenon, paying a big dividend on his acquisition, dropped a three-run bomb on his former team in the top of the sixth. We went on to win a big comebacker 8–7 behind Cal Koonce, and headed for Shea, hoping to rain on the Cubbies' parade.

The schedule had us facing the Cubs for three at home starting July 8, followed by three with Montreal, and then, on the 14th, heading to Chicago for another three-game set with Leo's bunch. Six games with the division-leading Cubs in nine days would get a player's attention, but the potential for a big swing one way or the other got the fans and the media in two major metros revved into overdrive. In practical terms, head-to-head confrontations usually resolve themselves as a big wash. Helping the hype was the vain, combative, aggressive Leo Durocher. Leo the Lip was a presence, large and occasionally bumptious. An average ballplayer in his day—one of his teammates on the Yankees, a fella named Babe Ruth, called him "the All-American Out"—but he was an astute manager. He had not invented baseball, but after his twenty-one years managing the Dodgers, Giants (1954 World Champs), and now the Cubs, Leo acted like he had. He was an old-school tough guy with a bedside manner like George Patton; he is credited with coining the phrase "Nice guys finish last," a derisive reference to Mel Ott, the Hall of Fame slugger turned "Nice Guy" manager of the Giants and resident of New Orleans, whose autograph hangs in my home in the Big Easy. You screw up for Leo and he would turn on you, big-time. There were things roiling in the Cubs clubhouse that were only revealed later. And it started with Leo Durocher.

The Cubs swaggered into Shea for a day game on July 8. Our five-game win streak had cut their lead in the NL East to five and a half games, the advantage the Cubs had enjoyed off and on for a couple of months. As he did so often, Jerry Koosman faced the other club's ace, future Hall of Famer Fergie Jenkins. In front of 55,000, an attendance record, Jenkins controlled the game, and held a 3–1 lead in the ninth inning when he induced Ken Boswell to loft what looked to be a catchable fly to short right center field. But Don Young misread it and got a late start, allowing the ball to fall for a leadoff double. An out later, Clendenon, batting for Bobby Pfeil, hit one to deep left center. Young went back hard and looked to make a nifty running catch, but when he banged into the wall, the ball fell free, dropped in for two bases, allowing the tying runs to reach second and third. Cleon, hitting around .350, hotter than a Times Square Rolex, ripped a double off the left field wall, and we were tied.

Leo had a choice. He could pitch to Ed Kranepool, who had homered earlier in the game, with Cleon representing the winning run at second; or walk the Krane and pitch to J. C. Martin. Leo chose option one, which gave them a base open, and room for Fergie to carefully pitch to Krane, which he was busy doing until Eddie dropped one into short left field and Cleon danced home. Unlike today's big leaguers, we did not attack our walk-off hero with shaving cream or sprays of soda. Instead we headed for our clubhouse to down a couple Rheingolds. Rheingold Beer bragged on our scoreboard about their ten-minute heads. In ten minutes, I beheaded a couple of them. It was a different story in the visitors' clubhouse.

Leo launched on poor Don Young with acid quotes to the writers and anyone else who would listen. "That kid in center field, two little fly balls. He just stands there watching one and gives up on the other. It's a disgrace." Of course, Leo had never played the outfield at Shea in the twilight. I could have told him how difficult it was with the high stands and the constantly moving background of fans for most fly balls. Even Santo, who knew better, joined the fray, jumping on Young, who sucked up an 0-for-4 hitting night as well. "He had a bad day at the bat, so he had his head down. He's worrying about his batting average and not the team. It's ridiculous. There's no way the Mets can beat us." In *Hamlet,* Queen Gertrude critiques some overacting in the play her son stages by saying, "The lady doth protest too much, methinks." I'm not suggesting panic, but the quotes from Leo and Santo seemed to reveal a tension that was turning in on itself. It was language and attitude that would never have happened in our clubhouse and we knew it. Clendenon went over to the Cubs' clubhouse to visit Ernie Banks and Billy Williams. He said you could have cut the tension with a knife.

The next night we strapped it on lefty Kenny Holtzman for three runs and an early shower while our ace, Tom Seaver, had a brush with perfection. With nine Ks through six innings, Seaver had no-no stuff and he smelled it. In the eighth with a 4–0 lead, Seaver paused to appreciate the moment; as he told Marino Amoruso, in his Hodges bio, *Gil Hodges: The Quiet Man,* "I paused between pitches to look the situation over. Fantastic. They were standing behind the last row of seats all the way down the left field line and right field line, and while I stopped to rub the ball, they were standing up and yelling their heads off." Heady time for sure, to be the cynosure of this moment and then to stop to take it all in. Wow. I had been replaced in right field for defense with Rod Gaspar. I knew exactly what Gil Hodges was thinking but that didn't keep me from hating it. For weeks now I had been working hard with Eddie Yost, fielding hundreds of fungos. The whole point was to make this defensive change unnecessary, but evidently Gil wasn't yet convinced. So, Gaspar was in right when Seaver got Santo on a fly ball to center and struck out Banks and Al Spangler. Perfection through eight.

In the ninth, Randy Hundley led off trying to bunt his way on. Sort of bush, in our minds. Swing the bat, man! You're a catcher. Who's gonna run it out for you? Fortunately, bunting was not something Hundley was any good at; Seaver fielded the bad bunt easily and threw him out. History was two outs away as rookie Jimmy Qualls came to bat in his eighteenth big league game. Qualls was a pretty good fastball hitter who had flied out to me and grounded hard to first base. He got a heater away from Seaver, and in a sad piece of anticlimax lined the cleanest single you will ever see to left center.

The bid was over. Seaver would throw five one-hitters for the Mets and wouldn't record a no-hitter until 1978 after his unpopular trade to the Cincinnati Reds. It is still a mystery to me why Seaver never could close the deal as a Met, but he has admitted that the pain from his near miss in 1969 never fully abated. "I couldn't measure the disappointment," Seaver confided later to writer Peter Golenbock. "Never, in any aspect of my life, in baseball or outside, had I experienced such a disappointment. At twenty-five, I was too old to cry." But I knew this wasn't true, and I knew I wasn't the only one.

Bill Hands handed us a 6–2 loss to salvage game three for the Cubs, and we then dropped another after the Expos came to town and whipped up on Jim McAndrew 11–4. Like a gift from heaven, we got rained out Saturday night, which left us strong and rested enough to take two from Montreal on Sunday. In game one, Kranepool notched a couple of RBIs, including the winning run in the eighth to make a winner of Koosman. In game two, I was in for Cleon, who had been having some ankle problems. And again, in this situation I helped out, singling in the seventh to break a tie and give us an 8–7 victory.

And now, on to Chicago. Wrigley Field was always one of my favorite places to play, especially when the wind was blowing out, making the "Friendly Confines" even friendlier. You could, literally, break your bat and still go deep. I know—I did it! Wrigley Field still lives today, with lights and tons of updated renovations. Yet, it was an old ballpark back then, with no lights. The visiting dugout was close to first base, so you had to listen to Ernie Banks declare every freakin' day, rain or shine, "It's a great day for baseball. Let's play two, let's play all day!" We'd ride Ernie about the time a few years earlier when he pulled that crap in the first of two games outdoors in Houston's pre-Astrodome, Colt Stadium. Ernie was talkin' about playing all day in 90 degrees and 90 percent humidity until the fourth inning of game one, when he went down with heat prostration. What was far in Wrigley Field was the walk from the dugout to the on-deck circle, leaving the fans ample time to get on your case. The bleacher bums yelled stuff that would make your mother cry, but none of that bothered me. I thought it was great. I'd always make eye contact and trade lines with them. Part of the game.

We loved playing day ball, get your game in and then put the rush on the bars on Rush Street. In fact, with the free time during this series, some of us caught *Easy Rider,* a biker movie made cheap that turned into a cult classic. The movie gave many of us our first long look at Jack Nicholson, who steals a few scenes before getting wasted. These days my favorite part of the movie comes when

Peter Fonda's and Dennis Hopper's characters hit New Orleans for Mardi Gras and heavy drugs in St. Louis Cemetery. I've lived in New Orleans since 1981, and enjoy their take on my city, especially the sound of the pilings being driven for what became the I-10 expressway through town.

We liked Wrigley, and we liked Chicago. What we didn't like was being shown up, and Ron Santo, the great third baseman, would do it. Like when the Cubs won game one, a pristine 1–zip shutout, Bill Hands over Seaver, Santo did his signature victory move: he jumped in the air and clicked his heels on the way to the clubhouse. As I mentioned, in that era, we barely acknowledged walk-off wins. Billy Williams, Santo's teammate, was of the old school. "I know a lot of guys on the other teams in the league didn't like that," he said. "They thought he was rubbing it in a little bit." Which might be an understatement. None of us liked it. Our veteran righty Don Cardwell, who had once thrown a no-hitter for the Cubs, said, "Santo was trying to show us up. We just weren't going to be shown up by anybody." Even Easy Ed Charles got a bit riled: Santo "was hot-dogging it and we thought it was a bush thing to do."

Maybe that's what prompted Hodges to get into the act. For several years, Gil played for Dodger teams that Leo managed, then for eight years he played against Giants teams that Leo managed. There must have been many opportunities for aggravation between the Gary Cooperish Hodges who spent World War II in combat and the cocksure Durocher who spent his World War II stateside dating starlets. "Gil and Leo used to yell back and forth to one another," said Joe Pignatano, one of Gil's closest friends, in an authorized Hodges biography by Tom Clavin and Danny Peary. "Gil never said he enjoyed managing against Leo, but he didn't have to. He also never said he didn't like him, but he knew Leo was a piece of crap." So, when a last-minute decision put all the day games from that series on television back to New York, Hodges noticed that there were a couple of TV headsets left in the dugout that they used in the pregame show. In 1951, when the Dodgers lost the NL championship in a famous three-game playoff to the Giants, Dodger partisans accused the Giants of scheming to steal the Dodger catcher's signs with a guy with binoculars who radioed them to the dugout. Back then, the accusation was all conjecture; since then, it seems to have been pretty well established that a signaling system had been rigged. Regardless, Gil put on one of the headsets and acted like he was hiding them under a towel and getting the catcher's signals from somewhere. He kept doing it until Leo finally acted like he saw him. As for the original incident, all I can say is that if you even caught a whiff that something like this was happening, you would have the catcher use multiple signs to thwart the opponent.

Whether or not Leo was annoyed by Hodges's gamesmanship, he was surely annoyed by the games that followed. Al Weis, who Hodges grabbed from the White Sox in 1968, still had a home in Chicago and was playing shortstop while Bud Harrelson did his two weeks of active duty in the army. With NBC broadcasting the game nationally, Weis was facing former Met Dick Selma with two Mets aboard. Weis, who hit a total of seven home runs in his 10 seasons in the big leagues, got hold of one and rode it out of Wrigley's Friendly Confines, evening up the series at one apiece.

That put a lot of attention on game three. If the Cubs won, each club would have taken a series on its home turf. Advantage: nobody. Instead, the great Ferguson Jenkins had a terrible outing, getting lit up for five runs, leaving without recording an out in the second inning. The lowly Mets had taken two series from the Cubs, lowered their lead to four games, and proved beyond question that we were for real.

We took that confidence to Montreal for our last series before the All-Star break where we'd split a four-game set with the Expos, winning the first one, losing the middle games by one run each, and taking the closer 4–3 in 10 innings. I had come off the bench and gotten a couple of hits in the earlier games and had three knocks in the finale, including a double in the 10th, when I scored the winning run from third on a ballsy two-out bunt single by Bobby Pfeil.

But I'm not sure any of us had our minds completely on baseball. On Wednesday, July 16, our last day in Chicago, Apollo 11 took off for the moon. It would take several days to get there, and those astronauts were never far from anyone's thoughts.

Meanwhile, at some point on Saturday afternoon, we first learned of what was being described as another tragedy to befall the Kennedy family. Senator Ted Kennedy had been involved in a car accident in a small community called Chappaquiddick, on the eastern end of Martha's Vineyard in Massachusetts. Kennedy had been injured, but a young woman named Mary Jo Kopechne had died. More than that we did not know, but all of us had vivid memories of the deaths of Jack and Bobby, and everybody was more somber than usual. But that didn't last too long. By Sunday we were back in our bubble, and in a great mood. We had won the game, we were flying home, most of us were going to get a three-day break—I felt like I was back in school, about to start Christmas recess.

Alas, our United charter, a French-built Caravelle jet, developed mechanical problems. The Caravelle was designed and constructed by Sud Aviation, a state-owned company that would go defunct by July 1970. Informed that fixing the jet would require only a small repair, we repaired to the airport lounge, where, over drinks, on a small TV, we watched with bursting pride as Neil Armstrong exited the lunar lander and made his "One small step for man, one giant leap for mankind." At that moment, I was standing next to Ed Kranepool, and we clinked glasses. The Mets weren't Number One . . . yet . . . but the USA was, and this feat proved it.

What a night! I was feeling pretty good. I had a couple of pops in me, Gil had given me some chances against the Expos and I had delivered, and Neil Armstrong and Buzz Aldrin were safely on the moon. Not lost on us, though, was the irony that while two astronauts walked on the moon, we couldn't get from Montreal to New York.

A few days later, Richie Allen agreed to return to the Phils. "This must be the greatest day in history," remarked his teammate Cookie Rojas. "The astronauts come down from the moon and Richie Allen comes down to earth."

When the Mets held their annual Banner Day Parade that year, hundreds of fans, as usual, brought homemade banners that they paraded across the field between games of a doubleheader. According to Joe Durso of *The New York Times*, among the 3,500 entries that year was one offered by Laura Joss, a fifteen-year-old from New Hyde Park on Long Island. ONE SMALL STEP FOR HODGES, her bedsheet canvas read, ONE GIANT LEAP FOR METKIND. Amen to that.

The Second Half

In my nine years of playing Major League Baseball, the All-Star Game was always something I watched on TV. In the history of the game, from 1933 to the present, there have been eighty-nine contests with the leagues virtually even, the AL winning forty-four and the NL forty-three, and two ties. But from 1963 through to 1982, the National League dominated, winning nineteen of twenty games. In 1969, the Mets sent Tom Seaver, Jerry Koosman, and Cleon Jones, and the NL rolled over the AL 9–3 in RFK Stadium. Cleon had a couple of hits, Koosman pitched a solid inning and two thirds, but Seaver sat it out. Tom came out of his near miss of perfection against the Cubs with some stiffness in his throwing shoulder. So, he took the All-Star break seriously by taking a break.

After his 1–0 loss to the Expos' Bill Stoneman on July 19, Tom had six days off before he went nine innings against Cincinnati in Shea, giving up eight hits, beating them 3–2 for his 15th win of the season. The day before, we took the Reds with three runs in the bottom of the eighth, including J.C. Martin's two-run HR. It was an encouraging start to a long stretch of games against the National League West that would turn bad quickly.

Houston was the problem. Historically, we never played well against them. Somehow, in our first triumphant season, it was even worse. Okay, we won two out of the first three against them at Shea early in the season. Then it got hard for us to even lose gracefully. The Astros beat us 10 times out of 12, many games by lopsided, football scores. Part of it was the atmosphere of the Astrodome where you'd play half the games; between the bouncy AstroTurf field and the roof overhead, we felt like we were playing canned baseball, and that we were canned vegetables. That might explain losing six of six in the Dome. But how did we lose four of six at home?

Looking at the numbers doesn't offer much explanation. The Astros, who would finish next to last in the NL West with an 81–81 record, had some good players in second baseman Joe Morgan, shortstop Denis Menke, third baseman Doug Rader, center fielder Jimmy "The Toy Cannon" Wynn, and a couple of good starters in Larry Dierker and Don Wilson. On the season, they would score fewer runs than us, while racking up a higher team ERA. In our games, however, they doubled our run output, outscoring us 78 to 36 in our season series. The guy we really helped make a star out of was reliever Fred Gladding. More on him later.

The Astros slipped into Shea Stadium for a doubleheader on July 30 and continued their dominance. In game one, Koosman pitched pretty well until trouble brewed in the top of the ninth. And I mean TROUBLE. As in, you got Trouble with a capital "T" and that rhymes with "P" and that stands for PHUCK! Sorry, that's my favorite line from *The Music Man,* and that's as close as I could get to making it fit. You can be sure there were a few four-letter F-bombs dropped in our dugout when we sailed into the ninth with a 5–3 lead and promptly watched the Astros strike for 11 runs, including a pair of grand slam home runs by Denis Menke and Jimmy Wynn. 1969 was the third time in the history of baseball that there were ever two grand slams in the same inning, and it's only happened five times in baseball history since 1969. (It was even more remarkable, on April 23, 1999 in L.A., since the grand slams were hit by the same player in the same inning, as Fernando Tatis of the Cardinals double tapped Chan Ho Park. Almost as odd, in 2007, Tatis and Chan Ho Park were both playing in New Orleans for the AAA Zephyrs. I don't recall any outward friction but they did refuse to sign the same ball, which would have been worth something.) Fred Gladding came in for the save, one of the six among his NL-best 29 saves that he recorded against us. But to add insult to injury, we turned Gladding into a hitting star. After thirteen big league seasons for the Tigers and Astros, Fred holds the major league record for the worst batting average above zero. Gladding had a career batting average of .016, going 1-for-33, and that one base hit was against the Mets' Ron Taylor in that awful game.

That was easily the worst inning we had against anybody that year. And then, like they didn't quite have our attention, the Astros produced a game two that was more of the same, another butt kicking where we provided the butts and the Houston Astros supplied the feet.

Gary Gentry, with stuff as good as Seaver and Koosman, was pitching in the top of the third of a nothing–nothing game with two outs and a runner at second. All of a sudden, he's pitching batting practice—single, walk, single, walk, triple, single, and within minutes it's 6–0 Astros. As they started handing us our asses once again, Gil Hodges started a slow burn. He pulled Gentry, and brought in

Ryan. Didn't make a difference. Houston's catcher John Edwards hit a clean double down the left field line, scoring Doug Rader from first. That prompted Gil to do something we had never seen before or ever would again.

Edwards's ball was extra bases all the way, but Cleon, with his bad feet, didn't exactly kill himself getting to the ball, nor was his throw from the outfield very impressive. Lobbed to third, Cleon's throw was described as "a balloon," by Vic Ziegel of the *New York Post,* with "the finish of a parachute jump," by Joe Donnelly of *Newsday,* but nobody noted that Shea's notoriously bad drainage system had left Cleon chasing the ball through water that covered his ankles. Upon which Hodges popped out of the dugout and with his hands in his back pockets, began a slow walk, stepping over the first base line, never on it. That's bad luck, everybody knows that. Ryan, awaiting a visit from what looked like a very pissed-off manager, watched as Hodges walked silently past. Gil then went by shortstop Bud Harrelson, who had done nothing wrong but who breathed a sigh of relief anyway. No, left field was Gil's objective. When he got within hailing distance of Cleon, he shouted, "Are you all right? What's the problem?" Whereupon, Cleon showed Gil how soggy the ground was. Hodges was unimpressed. "I don't think you went after that ball the way you should have," said Gil. "So you need to come out of this game." This moment started getting large. Cleon Jones was near the top of the league in hitting, and had never been the poster child for dogging it. He was a gamer, who played as hard as he could. But everyone saw the point Gil was making in the midst of that ugly run of baseball, especially Cleon, who quietly returned to the dugout, having been the not-entirely-deserving object of Hodges's lesson. Anything less than your best effort wouldn't flush, even if you were the team's best hitter in an ongoing race for the batting title, whether you were injured or not. Many years later, in 2003, at a talk at the Brooklyn Baseball Gallery in Coney Island,

Hodges's wife, Joan, added an interesting detail. When he returned home that night, the manager confessed that he hadn't gone out with the intention of pulling Cleon. "I didn't realize where I was until I passed the mound," he said with a shrug, "and then it was too late to go back."

I was the surprise replacement, and I would end up going 2-for-3 and scoring a couple of meaningless runs, but nothing would save us from an 11–5 loss, our second debacle of the day, against a team we would never defeat. When the Astros strapped an L on Seaver the next day, they left behind a beaten Mets team, now six and a half games behind a Cubs team that was still racking up wins at a sporty .612 clip.

While Cleon was resting and/or rehabbing his hamstring and his foot, I got the nod in left field. It was a huge opportunity that showed up as unmistakably as if the brand-new, fresh-off-the-road Oscar Mayer Wienermobile had pulled into Shea and began handing out free hot dogs. What I did, metaphorically, in four games was slop the mustard down the front of my jersey. I was a collective 0-for-10 on August 3, leaving runners all over the bases, when Gil, again, sent Shamsky up to pinch hit for me. Sham triggered a comeback 6–5 win over Atlanta in 11 innings. It proved to be the exception as the Mets floundered over the next 21 games, winning nine, and losing 12, concluding the run with three straight losses to Houston, who else?

And just like that, after securely holding down second place in the NL East for almost all of June, July, and the first thirteen days of August, we slipped into third, a game behind the Cardinals, a distant 10 games behind the division-leading Chicago Cubs. One hundred and eleven games into the season, the magic was slipping. Our tricks weren't working. Had we been found out? The image that comes to mind is of a guy working sleight of hand in front of a young audience whom none of the kids takes the misdirection and all of them point to his pocket where the coin had "disappeared." Meanwhile, the show moved elsewhere. Pittsburgh's Willie Stargell became the first human to launch one out of Dodger Stadium, off Alan Foster, measured at 500 feet. Jim Palmer of the Orioles no-hit the Oakland A's, a team that included Reggie Jackson, Sal Bando, and Rick Monday. On a farm northwest of New York City, Richie Havens opened the Woodstock music festival. He ended up playing for three hours because the traffic jam caused by the arrival of 500,000 people delayed the arrival of the other acts. Even in our bubble, we didn't seem so special.

California Dreaming

Fortunately, our stay in third place lasted only a day. Our wobble at the end of July and into August cost us some confidence, but we knew two things for sure. One, we wouldn't have to face that mighty Houston juggernaut anymore, and two, we were starting a twenty-game home-and-away run against the California teams, whom we had, so far, dominated, winning 12 and losing 2. Motivation is where you find it and matchups matter, don't believe otherwise. The Mets would win 15 out of the next 20. To be fair, San Diego was a bad team. They'd lose 110 games, and we'd win 11 of 12 against them. But the Dodgers, who'd win 85, and the Giants with 90 were both good. So, while our contemporaries were sloshing around in the mud and music of Woodstock, we got our teeth into a tight, six-game win streak opening with Seaver's complete game shutout 2–zip over San Diego. McAndrew, Koosman, and Cardwell would finish the Padres, 2–1, 3–2, 3–2.

Next came the Giants and Juan Marichal, who fashioned one of the most impressive losing efforts a fan could ever hope to see. The man with the high leg kick pitched into the bottom of the 14th, economically hurling a mere 150 pitches. But it wasn't good enough. With one out, Agee, who had gone 0-for-5 with three punch-outs, lined one into the visiting bullpen in left field, walking it off 1–0. Imagine pitching 13.1 innings of shutout at Shea and sucking up an L. The next day we lit up Gaylord Perry 6–0 behind McAndrew's two-hitter. My contribution to this auspicious run? Monumental moral support and a lot of slaps on the back. I got into the next game against San Fran when they started lefty Ron Bryant. I doubled in a run early and then tied the game at six with a two-out single off Frank Linzy, but Ken Henderson's RBI triple would win it for the Giants in the 11th.

Next came the Dodgers at Shea. They opened with a tough right-hander, Bill Singer. He was a hard thrower with a good sinker, one that he didn't mind improving with deft application of a little grease, a trick he learned from Drysdale. I got him early. With Garrett on, Singer tried to quick-pitch me and I took him deep, putting us on the path to a sweet 5–3 W. Cardwell had his nasty stuff the next night, and we won 3–2. Then we swept the series, with me going 2-for-3 and driving in four, including a three-run triple in the seventh, the winning runs in a comeback 7–4 win. Suddenly, we're on a roll and I'm relevant again.

Then off to San Diego where we open with an 8–4 win, my solo HR icing on the cake. Jim McAndrew is brilliant the next night, a nine-inning shutout, 3–0 Mets. I notch a pair of hits, only significant because my average blooms to .251, which would be my high-water mark. Dang it. Next night Koosman dominates, and we win 4–1, with Cleon driving in a pair, as I contribute a weak 0–4. Jonesy is hitting .350; I'm kissing .250 goodbye.

A hop up the coast and we're in San Francisco, *ding-ding*. That's the sound you hear the cable cars make and maybe Juan Marichal, too, no treat when he's ringing up our hitters. At Candlestick, his complete game 5–0 shutout evened things up—or did it? The great

Dominican won 21 games in '69, and led the league with a 2.10 ERA. Gaylord Perry was much sharper than when we saw him at Shea, but we still beat him again 3–2 on Clendenon's 10th-inning HR. In the next game, I started the scoring against the, by now, very familiar Mike McCormick with a two-run double, all Seaver would need in a complete game 8–0 shutout. The series ended with a 3–2 loss, though I drove in both Met runs, homering with a man on. Then, after a day of rest, we flew south, swept the Padres, and headed home.

Showdown

On August 27, 1969, when the outstanding lefty Ken Holtzman and his Chicago Cubs were rolled 6–3 by a very good Cincinnati Reds team, the Cubs completed a disturbing spell in which they lost seven of nine, and watched their lead in the National League East sink to two and a half games. Cubs fans were put on suicide watch. But then Chicago went on a five-game winning streak that restored the Cubs' lead to five games, and the wind coming out of the Windy City was an enormous cyclone of relief.

A slump is a journey, and like every journey, it begins with small steps. On September 3, the Cubs suffered a two-hit shutout against Cincinnati's Jim Maloney. No indignity there, but in their next game, at home in Wrigley, the Pirates' budding star Steve Blass did the damage with a four-hitter. Right after that, Ferguson Jenkins, seeking his 20th win, got roped into an early shower, losing 13–4. The losses went from rational, to improbable, and then to unlikely. Then they started to invent ways to lose, like the next day in extra innings when Pittsburgh got a win because the Cubs' peerless shortstop Don Kessinger booted a grounder. Four losses in a row, and their advantage was turning into sand in an hourglass. Officially, their lead was down to two and a half games; unofficially, they were in the weeds and coming our way.

When the Cubs faded down the stretch, a lot was laid on Leo Durocher, their manager, especially in New York, where he was a baseball fixture. His seventeen-year playing career started with the Yankees and ended with the Dodgers, and afterward he managed the Dodgers and the Giants until coming back for one last lap with the Cubs. He had an ego that Donald Trump would admire, and a starry lineup that any team would envy: the very capable keystone duo of Don Kessinger at short and Glenn Beckert at second, Hall of Famers Billy Williams in left, Ron Santo at third, and Ernie Banks at first; and admirable pros Jim Hickman, a former Met, in right, and Randy Hundley behind the plate. That lineup played almost every day and Leo was wearing out his four-man starting rotation with Fergie Jenkins, Ken Holtzman, Dick Selma, and Bill Hands. By August, major league players wear down; the Cubs' starters had to have been feeling it. The Mets under Hodges platooned up and down the lineup; he spread the load, Leo did not. There was another difference, as argued by our backup catcher in an interview. "Never once did I see Gil Hodges react in a way to cause panic," said J. C. Martin. "Never once!" We could pull the dumbest play in the world, but he'd never show panic. And he instilled that in his players.

As a sportscaster in New Orleans, I remember Bum Phillips when he was coaching the Saints talking about Tom Landry of the Cowboys. Bum said, "He could take his'n and beat your'n and take your'n and beat his'n." I think that's what J.C. was saying about Gil.

When the Cubs showed up at Shea on September 8 with their two-and-a-half-game lead, they were obviously limping. Their ace, Ferguson Jenkins, was faltering with a sore arm. Durocher, with all the tact of a bouncer working the door at a two-bit bar, had called Holtzman "a gutless Jew." The *Chicago Tribune,* in an oral history on the Cubs' slide, quoted Leo, whose crudeness is more presidential today. "I never saw anything like it in my life. Our offense went down the toilet, the defense went down the drain and I'm still looking for the pitching staff. I could have dressed nine broads up as ballplayers and they would have beaten the Cubs." Left-hander Rich Nye, who today is a veterinarian specializing in rare birds, talked to me about his rare bird of a manager. "It got to be a joke the way Leo would telephone the bullpen and tell them to get Phil Regan up." (Regan pitched in 71 games and saved 17.) "It's like he forgot the rest of us." Somebody—whether it was Leo or his starting pitcher, Bill Hands—concluded that a show of bravado was called for, and decided it was time to play the intimidation game. When Tommie Agee led off the bottom of the first inning, the message came wrapped in a fastball, aimed straight at his coconut. That got everybody's attention. I recall Seaver on the top steps of our dugout, barking, "You don't want to play that game." And it *was* a bad idea—we weren't going to be so easily cowed, and none of the Cubs hitters wanted to get knocked down in turn by our power arms. If Seaver had been pitching, the Cubs might have gotten away with a low bridger or one thrown behind them, but Koosman was on the mound, and he had the heart of an assassin. When Ron Santo led off the second, he barely got his left elbow up in time to keep Koozie's 90 mph response from drilling him in the earhole. To Ralph Kiner, one of the Met broadcasters, "It sounded like Koosman broke his arm." Santo, a tough guy, stayed in the game, but went down to first base a changed man. That ended the knockdowns, and maybe more than that. Agee would homer and later score the winning run after his double, and we would win 2–1.

The next night, September 9, we lit up the suddenly ineffective Jenkins, and rode Seaver home for a 7–1 win. The Cubs crawled out of New York hanging on by their fingernails to a fragile half-game lead. It wouldn't survive twenty-four hours. Smack in the middle of a ten-game win streak, the Mets would take a pair from Montreal, 3–2 in 12 innings on Ken Boswell's walk-off single and then a runaway 7–1 win in game two behind Nolan Ryan's sixth victory. Now we had the lead in the National League East, a lead we would never surrender.

Earlier in the summer, Richard Dozer, a former Chicago sportswriter, suggested to Durocher that he occasionally rest his players. In response, Leo invited Dozer into the locker room and bellowed, "Does anyone want to come out of the lineup because they are tired?" Durocher yelled, "Beckert! Are you tired?" "Nope," said second baseman Glenn Beckert. "Hey Kessinger?"—SS Don Kessinger— "Is the heat getting to you?" "No Leo, I'm not tired." And so it went around the clubhouse. But like the leaders in a stock car race on the NASCAR circuit, the Cubs had been out front pushing the hot summer air.

I was even quoted, at length, on the subject in the *Tribune* piece. "We were ingenues. We had that wonderful, clear-minded innocence of not having the responsibility of winning it, of not having to doubt ourselves if we stumbled." In the most candid comments coming out of the Cubs clubhouse, according to third baseman Ron Santo, it wasn't just the summer heat in Chicago they were feeling. "Players or managers will always say, 'I don't read the papers or look at the scoreboard.' That's baloney. We went to the West Coast with an eight-game lead. I recall that we lost our first two ball games on the West Coast, and the Mets won their first two. Every time we would go into the ballpark on the West Coast to take batting practice, their game was over and the Mets won. It was just more and more pressure." The Cubs never lost two straight on that West Coast trip. But with us winning three out of every four games in our maddening run, it had to feel like that to Santo.

Once the Cubs lost their lead, they lost their fire. They would drop eight in a row, lose 11 of 12, and find themselves trailing by four and a half as the calendar evaporated. We clinched the division title on the 24th of September, but not before some incredible stuff went down.

Those key wins over the Cubs were part of a 10-game win streak that included a twin bill in Pittsburgh that we swept with scores of 1–0 and 1–0. The scores are not as remarkable as how we got the two runs that earned us two wins. Koosman would go the route in the opener and drive in the only run he needed. Koosman had made some progress as a hitter, moving from awful to just short of mediocre. Don Cardwell was a good hitter and drove in his only run while going the minimum five innings for the win. That could not have happened too many times in the history of baseball, that two pitchers drove in the only runs they needed to win a pair of games on one day. You can look it up.

We won game three in Pittsburgh when I hit a grand slam off right-hander Chuck Hartenstein. From there it was off to St. Louis for a makeup game with the Cardinals. In another head-scratcher of a win for us, I had the best day I ever had as a hitter.

Steve Carlton got the start and was otherworldly with his stuff. He started out by striking out Bud Harrelson swinging and Amos Otis on a called third strike, but Tommie Agee reached on an error and Donn Clendenon singled. Carlton then ended the inning by striking me out swinging.

Gary Gentry pitched for us, and he had his good stuff. In the third, after Carlton set down Charles, Grote, and Gentry, all on strikes, the Cards took a 1–0 lead, setting the stage for some heroics. Clendenon started the inning with a walk, but Lefty quickly set me up with two strikes. Deciding against wasting a pitch, he challenged me with a fastball, which I deposited in the left field seats for a two-run shot that put us up 2–1. After the homer, Carlton struck out the side.

By my third at bat, the Cards had restored a 3–2 lead, and Carlton was continuing at his astonishing pace. He notched me again on my third at bat, and showed no signs of stopping when he faced me in the eighth. With one out and Tommie Agee on first, Carlton once again got me to 0–2. But then he came after me with a pretty good slider, which I drilled on a line over the left field wall, right into the area where the Cardinals have a batting cage and a pitching machine. Ironically, before the game, our broadcaster Ralph Kiner, the Hall of Fame slugger, and I went to that area, and Ralph fed me some balls and worked on my hitting.

In setting the strikeout record at 19, Carlton eclipsed a mark jointly held by Sandy Koufax, Bob Feller, and Don Wilson. He struck out the side four times, including the ninth, which he had to do to set the record. "It was the best stuff I ever had," Carlton said after the game. "When I had nine strikeouts, I decided to go all the way. But it cost me the game because I started to challenge every batter."

Carlton should not have lost that game with the kind of stuff he had, and I should not have taken him deep twice or maybe at all. He should have won, and the Cubs, playing the lowly expansion Expos, should also have won. But he didn't and the Cubs didn't, and our lead increased to four and a half games. But that's the sort of thing that happened on our way to winning the National League East. On our way to a piece of immortality. When reality seemed to defy logic on a daily basis.

The real capper was when we closed the regular season in Chicago. The cranks in Wrigley, an old-time baseball term for fans, had planned to drape a huge, purple funeral crepe over the visiting dugout. Which they did. But the fact that we had iced the Cubs weeks before, clinching the regular season division title, the crepe and all that crap was hilarious, but irrelevant. We couldn't have given less of a shit what the Cub fans, the Cubs, and Ron Santo clicking his heels down the left field line were up to. We were on our way to Atlanta and the National League Championship Series.

The beautiful thing about getting somewhere you have never been before is that you never get ahead of yourself. Each day is separate. You live in the here and now, and it couldn't have been more exciting.

The Playoff Against the Braves

On September 24, we clinched our division at Shea Stadium in front of 56,000 fans. It's incredible that all our celebrations in 1969 happened in front of our fans at Shea. Gary Gentry, our rookie right-hander, outpitched Steve Carlton. This was Lefty's first outing after setting the strikeout record, and he wasn't nearly as sharp. With Bud Harrelson and Tommie Agee aboard, Donn Clendenon homered. Ed Charles, thirty-six years old, a gentleman poet who spent ten good seasons in the minors before starting his big league career, also homered. We carried a 6–0 lead into the ninth. With two on, Joe Torre, the man who many experts thought "might have made a pennant contender out of the Mets" if the team had coughed up enough meaningful young talent in the spring, came to the plate. He drilled a hard grounder to Harrelson at short, who started a slick 6–4–3 double play. And the pennant race was over. Tim McCarver, the Cardinals' catcher and later one of our better baseball color commentators, was on deck. He said that Carlton had sworn that the Mets weren't going to clinch against him, but we did. The fans at Shea went berserk.

Metaphorically, Koppett would describe the surge onto the field in more historic literature, "like deranged lemmings, like the mob attacking the Bastille, like barbarians scaling the walls of ancient Rome, like maddened initiates in some Dionysian rite . . . driven, however, by pure joy, by ecstasies beyond hope of control."

And that was just for winning the division title. There was no trophy for winning the East. All we had won was the right to face the winner of the National League's western division, and with a week to go, that could have been one of three teams. The Atlanta Braves sat in first place on the 25th of September, a game and a half in front of the San Francisco Giants. Though none of us was foolish enough to publicly express which team we would prefer to play in the best-of-five League Championship series, I would have loved it to be the Giants, because of everything we shared in New York lineage and history. The Cincinnati Reds, who owed me a grand slam home run from my rookie season, were the third team in the mix, three games off the lead.

It would, eventually, be Atlanta winning the West by three games, a team we had beaten eight out of twelve regular season games, and outscored as well. Wonderful stats that meant zip going into the best-of-five series. The Braves' pitching was strong, featuring the Hall of Fame knuckleballer Phil Niekro, righty Ron Reed, and a bunch of other guys, most of them right-handed. Under Hodges's platoon system, that meant I'd be watching a lot of baseball. The Braves' lineup would get your attention with Hank Aaron (44 home runs—97 RBIs), Orlando Cepeda (22 home runs—88 RBIs), and Rico Carty (.342 BA—16 home runs) and a legion of other good hitters. With the first two games in Atlanta, they'd have the chance to open a quick lead.

We left our two boys, both toddlers, with our best friends, Charlie and Gertie Blansfield, so that Cecilia could travel with me to Atlanta. Charlie was a detective on the job in Nassau County. After we moved to Syosset, Long Island, they had treated Cecilia and me like family and that love was returned by us.

In Atlanta, we stayed at a brand-new Marriott Hotel in what they were beginning to call the New South. While in line for breakfast on the morning of Game One, two finely dressed and perfectly quaffed "Southern Ladies" regaled each other with tales prompting one "Well, I declare!" after another. More like, "Well, I dee-CLAY-er." Adding a syllable while each succeeding declaration reached a slightly higher pitch. Cecilia and I smiled at each other and rolled our northern eyes. It came to be said that the "real south" was in any direction you headed out of Atlanta, but we thought we were in line for the casting call for a remake of *Gone with the Wind*. Later I learned that the Clark Gable–Vivian Leigh epic had amongst its investors Joan Whitney Payson and her brother Jock. Mrs. Payson had attended the gala premiere in Atlanta thirty years before.

Hoping not to be gone with the wind after the NL playoffs, we nonetheless found ourselves in a seesaw game: we went up by two, then they went up by one. In the fourth, with Kranepool and Grote on, Buddy Harrelson rolled one down the first base line by Cepeda that went for a two-run triple. But Seaver, who was 3–0 versus the Braves in the regular season, was off his game. He got touched by Tony Gonzalez for a tying home run in the fifth and a go-ahead shot by Aaron in the seventh.

Their lead disappeared quickly. In the top of the eighth, Wayne Garrett doubled to left against Niekro, and Jonesy promptly singled him home. That tied the game at 5. Cleon stole third on a pickoff attempt by the Braves' catcher Bob Didier. When Kranepool rolled a slow grounder to first, Jones broke for home. Cepeda should have had him easily, but he bounced the ball by Didier, and we were back on top by a run. With Boswell at second and Krane at first, Grote's groundout moved the runners to second and third. With Seaver coming up, Niekro walked Harrelson to intentionally load the bases. Hodges countered by sending J.C. Martin up to pinch hit. Martin singled to center, which would have been good enough for the lead. But the ball skimmed past Gonzalez in center, clearing the bases. Seaver had been less than terrific, but it was the Braves who had cracked, and we tucked Game One into our back pocket 9–5.

In Game Two, the Braves' defense was shaky again and the Mets' left-handed lineup made them and their starter, Ron Reed, pay with a run in the first, three in the second, two each in the third and fourth, and one in the fifth. Atlanta committed three errors and our left-handed bats cashed them in for a 9–1 lead heading to the bottom of the fifth. Our left-handed pitching was tough, too, in the opening four innings, but Koosman, unused to this sort of lead in his first playoff appearance, stumbled in the fifth, giving way to Ron Taylor after Aaron's three-run blast and Clete Boyer's two-run single ended his day. Taylor took us to the seventh, then gave way to Tug McGraw, whose three-inning save sealed the deal 11–6.

The New York Mets had rolled the Braves in their place. Now we headed to Shea up 2–zip, one win shy of a ticket to the World Series. I had witnessed some pretty amazing offense with only a scare to show for it. A scare in 1969 baseball parlance was either a pitcher who warmed up but didn't get into the game or, in my case, a pinch hitter who was kneeling on deck as the third out was made. I got my "scare" and that was it.

A real scare had come in the top of the seventh after Tommie Agee walked, stole second, then moved to third on Garrett's long fly ball. With Cleon hitting, Agee came down the line intent on stealing home. Cleon, unaware, ripped a line drive that shot right by Agee's face. Had it hit him, it could have killed him. It missed for a foul ball strike. Jonesy then followed with a home run over the left field fence, and we left Atlanta with two of our most important players shaken but alive.

Because playing baseball absorbs so much of your being, this playoff experience made everything seem new. You were wearing new clothes, new shoes, breathing new air, not thinking beyond the reach of your nose. You knew you felt like a million bucks. My juices were flowing full bore even though I hadn't played an inning of baseball and likely would not, with Pat Jarvis, another right-hander, slated for Game Three at Shea. The only sure thing was that I would have a good seat.

Shea was packed, and the city was jumping. We were the story and from where I was sitting, the only thing missing was better service. In today's premium seating behind home plate, you can order drinks and food. Back then, you had to run into the dugout to get a Coke or a candy bar but you didn't want to miss a pitch.

Gary Gentry, a fearless rookie with incredible stuff, was on the mound. But with Tony Gonzalez on first, Bad Henry—as Sandy Koufax had dubbed Henry Aaron—jumped a fastball. Hank's monster two-run blow put us down right out of the chute. Still two runs didn't seem all that much of a lead, if Gentry would settle down.

That didn't happen. In the top of the third, Gonzalez led off with a single and Aaron doubled. With men on second and third, none out, and Rico Carty batting, Hodges phoned the bullpen and got Nolan Ryan up. Three pitches later, on a 1–1 count, Carty ripped a deep, loud foul down the left field line. Hodges had seen enough. It was one of those moments when Gil knew that Gentry didn't have it and maybe every other Met fan did, too, but only Hodges had the balls to act. In the middle of Carty's at bat, Gil walked to the mound and called for Ryan. "I had only thrown about ten or twelve pitches," Nolan told me recently. "I was barely warmed up. I was surprised as anybody when Gil brought me in."

If you were Rico Carty, you knew what was coming your way. Ryan's fastball was not yet legendary, not yet known as "Ryan's Express" after the Frank Sinatra war movie of 1965, *Von Ryan's Express*. These were the days before speed guns started putting numbers to pitches, but Nolan's heater had to be upper-90s gas, and his curveball was pretty violent when Nolan had the feel for it. Anyway you looked at it, this was a big at bat and Carty was ready.

With two strikes, Carty lined a couple of fastballs down the left field line foul, and not by much. But Nolan brought a little more express and struck out Carty. After walking Cepeda intentionally to load the bases, Nolan struck out Clete Boyer looking, then got Didier on a harmless fly ball to end the threat. It was one of those baseball situations where, if you got through it, guys would look at one another on the bench and make those "wow!" faces and then talk about it years later. Hodges had made a gutsy move—only in retrospect can you say that bringing Nolan Ryan would have been a high-percentage move—but Hodges had taken chances all season long. All you could do was marvel.

Like two heavyweights exchanging haymakers, we went to trading home runs with the Braves. Bottom of the third, Agee launched a solo shot and got us within a run. The next inning, Ken Boswell sent one into the right field bullpen with his buddy Shamsky aboard that gave us a 3–2 lead. Top of the fifth, Cepeda reached Ryan for a two-run blow and Atlanta nudged in front 4–3. It was a short-lived lead. In the bottom of the inning, with Ryan aboard on a base hit, Wayne Garrett drove one out down the right field line. The 5-4 lead eventually grew into a 7–4 lead and finally a victory, as Nolan finished the game for the win. We were on our way to the World Series. During the three-game sweep, our left-handed platoon outscored the Braves 27 to 15, out-homered them six to five, outhit them .327 to .255.

There was champagne, of course, and more craziness on the field by the fans. We had watched some of the earlier games in the American League Championship Series. My boyhood team, the Baltimore Orioles, rolled the Minnesota Twins 11–2 to sweep them after squeaking out one-run extra inning wins in the first two games.

This was going to be special. Even after our left-handed platoon had outhit the Braves, Gil Hodges reminded us that the Orioles started two superb lefties in Mike Cuellar and Dave McNally, so the right-handed platoon better be ready. It would be strange. We wouldn't meet up until October 11 in Baltimore's Memorial

Stadium. I hadn't played an inning since October 2, the last day of the regular season when fewer than ten thousand disappointed Cubs fans turned out at Wrigley. But don't worry about the nine-day layoff, it was only Game One of the World Series.

The World Series

Although the results of the annual All-Star Game proved that the National League had more skilled players, the results of the previous ten World Series showed a more even balance, but still a definitive six-to-four advantage in titles for the NL. The team we were facing in the Series, the Baltimore Orioles, owned one of the AL's four titles, and the nucleus of that squad that swept the Dodgers in 1966 made up the core of the powerful '69 team, which had won 109 games and swept a solid Twins team to reach the Series. The highly decorated Robinsons were the leaders: Frank, the tough right fielder, had won the Triple Crown in 1966, and was the only man to win MVP in both leagues; the affable Brooks, who was awarded the MVP in 1964, had earned the tenth of what would turn out to be sixteen Gold Gloves for his play at third base in 1969. Also wearing a ring from that '66 team was the slugger Boog Powell; a very capable second baseman named Davey Johnson (who, nearly two decades later, would earn a place of honor in Mets history as manager of the 1986 World Series winners); the shortstop Mark Belanger and the center fielder Paul Blair, both slick defensive wizards; and excellent starters Jim Palmer and Dave McNally. Reinforcing those troops were the crafty left-handed starter Mike Cuellar, who had come over from Houston in a midwinter deal and promptly won 23 games and a share of the Cy Young Award with Denny McClain; the excellent leadoff man Don Buford; and in the dugout, the canny, cantankerous manager, Earl Weaver.

Our arrival left something to be desired. The Mets checked into the Sheraton-Belvedere Hotel, a beautiful Beaux-Arts Baltimore landmark that was built in 1902 and was beginning to show its age. That was no excuse for the disappointing service the team received. I heard the staff seemed entirely unprepared for a large group of professional athletes and their wives who might want breakfast and room service. Nothing seemed to work. On the morning of the day he was to pitch in the opening game of the World Series, Tom Seaver waited forever in the hotel dining room to see a menu. He finally gave up, and he and Bud Harrelson headed for Memorial Stadium and ordered sandwiches in the clubhouse. You're welcome. I was staying at home with my Mom and Dad and the service was great.

Growing up in the Baltimore area, I was familiar with Memorial Stadium. I played in an amateur all-star game there when I was sixteen, knocking a homer over the 309-foot sign down the left field line. More recently, I worked out with the Orioles, wearing their gear, taking batting practice against their hard-throwing young lefty Steve Barber, and giving their scouts one more look-see at what I could do. It would have been nice to play for my hometown. This is where I saw my first major league game, in 1954, the team's first season in Crab Town. Vic Wertz, the power-hitting first baseman, hit a home run. That turned out to be Vic's only home run for the Orioles. He was soon traded to Cleveland, who won the American League title. In Game One of the World Series against the Giants, Vic walloped a drive to the deepest part of the Polo Grounds, 420 feet to straightaway center. On the dead run, Willie Mays made an over-the-shoulder catch, arguably the greatest catch ever made, captured for eternity with the same bulky stop-action camera that would record my catch in just a few days.

My first chance to make a great World Series catch of my own came right away, in the bottom of the first in Game One, on Tom Seaver's second pitch, and I blew it completely. I'll admit it—the moment was overwhelming me. Adrenaline overload, anxiety, excitement, the presence of family members in the stands, and somewhere, roaming around, the kid who cheered for Vic Wertz, the same kid who started this whole baseball odyssey with Dad throwing me pitches, now here in the World Series! Breathing heavily, I watched Seaver go into his motion. Guessing fastball, Don Buford launched one deep to right field.

All that practice, all those line drives from Eddie Yost, all the confidence I had built up, failed. Trouble from the get-go. On the replays, I look like C-3PO, the golden droid from *Star Wars,* running back on the ball, or, maybe, the Tin Woodsman from *The Wizard of Oz* looking for his oil can. Stiff, unsure, I never made any connection at all with the ball in flight. Arriving late to the wall, I turned to face the ball, and threw myself into a leap that was as poorly timed as it was off target. The ball passes just outside my glove and lands over the fence, and I land on my keister. I should have caught it, but instead it's 1–0 O's.

I'm freaking livid. Nobody out, we're already down a run to the heavily favored Orioles. Buford is halfway through his home run trot. As he goes by Harrelson at short, he cracks, "You ain't seen nothin' yet." It's Al Jolson's line from *The Jazz Singer.* I was a huge Jolson fan, knew all the words from singing along with my Dad's record albums. Buford had it right, but not for the reason he thought.

I came back to our dugout yapping, "I shoulda caught it." Kranepool's hardass New Yorker response landed like a slap upside my head: "Shut the fuck up and get the next one." We would, all of us. The Orioles would win that day, but we came back, and defense was one of the keys. Look online at the highlights of the '69 Series. We made a whole bunch of damned good defensive plays, and I would get my shot at redemption for the one I let get away.

For more than a month, we had been playing incredible baseball, capped by the sweep of the Braves. Now, in our first encounter with the Orioles, we not only got beat, but suddenly lost our swagger. Seaver hadn't been sharp, and I wasn't the only one who had played nervous. But in the clubhouse afterward, Gil Hodges had said the most sobering, supportive, entirely reasonable thing a manager could say to his young, recently accomplished baseball team. "You don't have to be anything more than what got you here," said Gil, showing no greater concern than getting the clubhouse guy to grab him a beer. In other words, he didn't want us thinking we had to swell up to something bigger than life to come back from a game down. In life's rearview mirror, it was pitch-perfect.

And wasting no time, come back we did. For Game Two we had Jerry Koosman, as cool and tough as the situation demanded. To face the O's lefty Dave McNally, another 20-game winner, we ran our right-handed platoon out there again. Donn Clendenon got us on the board with a solo opposite field home run to lead off the fourth, and it stayed one–nothing until the seventh when Paul Blair, the former Met farmhand, singled, stole second, and with two outs scored on Brooks Robinson's single to center.

While I had quietly sucked up a 0-for-4, with two outs in the top of the ninth, Ed Charles and Grote hit back-to-back singles. McNally was still in there with Al Weis coming up. One-for-three on the day with a single to center his first time up, the light-hitting Weis—he hit just .215 on the year—rewarded Hodges's confidence with a two-out single. Charles scored, giving us a 2–1 lead. Gil knew Weis from the American League and Al's time with the Chicago White Sox. Gil felt like Weis could "do some things to help you win," and he was right again.

Koosman was cruising, but with two outs in the bottom of the ninth, Koozie walked Frank Robinson and Boog Powell. I'm still in right field, which felt like a victory to me. I had worked all year, taking hundreds of line drives, ground balls, to my left, to my right, in front of me and over my head to become a better fielder and, in the final six weeks of the regular season Hodges had responded, shelving his standard defensive move to Rod Gaspar for me in right. When the O's manager, Earl Weaver, pinch ran Merv Rettenmund for Frank Robinson, Hodges came out and got Koosman, replacing him with Ron Taylor, a sinker/slider guy who didn't have Koosman's velocity. Knowing that a hitter might be more likely to send one of Ron's pitches down the line, Charles moved a little closer to the third base line. Good thing because Brooks Robinson hit him a tricky hopper that he grabbed. Looking initially for the force at third, Ed changed his mind and flipped it to first for the out. "A lot of people make a big fuss about that play," Ed would say later, "but it wasn't anything special." Just a world-class in-between hopper that you see messed up all the time, interrupted by a change of plans in the middle, maybe aided by Brooks Robinson being not so fleet afoot. Charles's throw to first was perfect, and we had split the first two in Baltimore.

Back to New York for Game Three. In Baltimore, the stands were full of my relatives with tickets I had bought for them, to the tune of about $1,000. They wanted me to do well, but for the Orioles to win. I understood that. My home in Syosset would be full, with my folks and my grandmother Agnus, who was married to my Chinese step-grandfather, Arthur. They would all be in the stands at Shea with a host of top-tier celebrities, including Louis Armstrong, Jackie Kennedy, and the most authentic Mets fan of them all, Pearl Bailey.

At the first game in Baltimore, Spiro Agnew, the former Maryland governor and soon to be disgraced vice president, threw out the first pitch. In the first game in New York, the first pitch was thrown out by Joe DiMaggio. He was sitting in the first row to the left of our dugout as we looked out at the field. Our trainer, Gus Mauch, who had worked with DiMaggio when they were both New York Yankees in the glory days, leaned out of the dugout and gave Joe this big, can-you-freakin'-believe-it wave. Joe gave Gus the same response he reportedly gave Marilyn Monroe, with her star on the rise as they stepped off an airplane in New York right after their marriage. "Joe," she gushed, "have you ever seen such a crowd?" "Well, yes I have," Joe understated.

That was the rocking, roiling environment at Shea Stadium into which the Orioles sent Jim Palmer, their excellent young right-hander, to face our sterling rookie, Gary Gentry. Palmer had movie-star good looks and a life story that only Hollywood could do justice to. First, he was adopted as a kid; his name comes from his adopted mother's second husband. During the course of developing into one of the hardest-throwing prospects in America, Palmer played on a summer league team in South Dakota. Driving home with a friend, They went off the road and flipped a couple of times. Palmer injured his knee. Eventually he would require surgery, but the Orioles, unaware of the wreck and injury, gave Palmer a $50,000 bonus to sign with them. His career went straight up from there, making the big club in 1965 as a nineteen-year-old, and beating Sandy Koufax in the World Series the following year as the Orioles swept the Dodgers. (If you're ever in a sports trivia contest, a pretty reliable question to ask is: Who was the last pitcher to defeat Sandy Koufax?) But arm troubles in 1968 threatened to derail Palmer's most promising career, to the point where he considered giving up pitching and trying to make it as a position player. So serious was his prognosis that the Orioles left Jim unprotected in the expansion draft after the 1968 season, and no other major league team took him. Back then, the conventional wisdom decreed that pitchers should try to throw through the pain, which Jim did in the winter leagues in Puerto Rico. Like magic, the pain went away, and Palmer rejoined the Orioles in midseason and racked up a 16–4 record.

With that drama behind him, Palmer faced Tommie Agee, leading off the bottom of the first. Tommie took Palmer deep, an uncommon event in Jim's career. But if that was unusual, the bottom of the second would be positively bizarre. With two out, and facing the bottom third of the order, Palmer walked Grote, gave up a single to Harrelson, and then surrendered a two-run double to Gentry, who had hit a mere .081 on the year. Behind 3–0, the Orioles could have immediately closed the gap in the fourth, when Frank Robinson and Boog Powell reached base with one out. Brooks Robinson struck out, leaving Frank Robinson on third. Elrod Hendricks, the O's catcher, an average hitter with a bit of pop, then smashed a liner to deep left center. Tommie Agee, ranging from right center to left center, running hard the whole way, at the last moment lunged on his backhand to make the catch and ended the threat. From the dugout, we could see the ball hanging halfway out of his mitt, so near to disaster for us.

With two out in the seventh, Gentry, now holding a 4–0 lead, finally wobbled and walked the bases full. Hodges went to the pen for Nolan Ryan. After his hurry-up appearance in the playoffs against Atlanta, Ryan was ready. But so was Paul Blair. The one-time Met prospect lined Ryan's heater into the gap in deep right field. Blair had to have been thinking three bases, no one had ever hit an inside-the-park grand slam home run in a World Series.

But almost like the Hendricks catch run in reverse, Agee galloped hard the other way and snared Blair's drive. Agee said this one was easier for him because it was to his glove side. From my perspective, nothing about diving for a ball is easy, as Agee, coming from left center field to right center, banging his glove once or twice, laid out and made the play. With two outs in two different situations, with five runners on base, Tommie Agee had made two catches on drives that by all rights should have gone bouncing off the wall. After Kranepool's home run in the eighth, we would win it 5–0. The Orioles had to feel snakebitten as two, big run-scoring opportunities were yanked from their hands by Tommie Agee. The chips were falling our way.

Fly Your Flag

While we were in the midst of a pretty thrilling World Series, a lot of the country had its mind on another matter. A group called the New Mobilization Committee to End the War in Vietnam had called for a national Moratorium—a stoppage of all activities to protest the war—and in cities and on campuses, millions of people heeded the call.

In Manhattan, there were rallies in Bryant Park and at Columbia University. Tens of thousands gathered on Boston Common, in Grant Park in Chicago, and in Golden Gate Park in San Francisco. Huge crowds stood in silent vigil before the Capitol in Washington. In Great Britain, a Rhodes Scholar named Bill Clinton organized demonstrations at Oxford.

The massive protests even managed to invade our baseball bubble. New York City mayor John Lindsay, an opponent of the war who was in the midst of a desperately close election campaign, called for the U.S. flag to be flown at half-staff. It was a bit of a stunt, since mayors don't have the authority to order flags flown at half-staff, but that didn't stop Baseball Commissioner Bowie Kuhn from snapping at the bait. He ordered the flags flown in the normal way. Even though he didn't have any more authority over the question than Lindsay did. Meanwhile, outside Shea Stadium, a group calling itself Mets Fans for Peace handed out leaflets protesting the war. On the cover was a picture of Tom Seaver and a news clipping in which he called the U.S. involvement in the war "perfectly ridiculous" and said if the Mets went on to win the Series, he would buy an ad in *The New York Times* saying, "If the Mets can win the World Series, then we can get out of Vietnam." After the game, Seaver said he had not been in favor of the pamphlets, and that he'd "been used." He said he would do something after the Series.

"Whatever I do, it will be on my own, not with any group, just as an American citizen." That happened on New Year's Eve, when Tom paid for an ad in *The New York Times* calling for Americans to pray for peace in Vietnam. Can't argue with that.

Turning Point

People talk about a pregame atmosphere; Game Four had it in spades. Both teams were serious; the Orioles were angry for finding themselves in their predicament, and we were all business. If we were anxious, it was more about our eagerness to see what would come next. Clendenon was like a man possessed, totally in his element, exuding confidence that seemed completely authentic and contagious.

Both Seaver and Cuellar, the famously superstitious Cuban with a mean screwball, came out and got down to work. You can tell a lot about this game by one statistic—2:33. That was the rather short length of time this taut, tight game took to play. Both pitchers got on the rubber and threw. They were sharp; they challenged the hitters. Seaver gave up six hits, Cuellar seven, but that one extra hit made all the difference—a solo home run by Donn Clendenon leading off the second. Giving up one run usually doesn't affect a team very much, but you could tell that with every inning that passed when the Orioles didn't score, Clendenon's lone run loomed all the larger. Once, commenting on the shadows that fell across left field in the old Yankee Stadium, our coach Yogi Berra produced one of his famous malaprops: "It gets late early out there." By midafternoon, it was getting late for the Orioles.

Both teams had chances, getting men on without managing a clutch hit. Cuellar left after seven, but his successor, Eddie Watt, set down the side in order in the eighth. Hodges let Seaver hit; he certainly had the option of sending up Kranepool or Shamsky and seeing if they could do something that would bring us an insurance run, but I don't think Gil entertained the idea. He was going to keep riding his big horse.

Paul Blair began the ninth by lofting a fly ball to me in right. Just two outs to go. But then Frank Robinson singled, and then Boog Powell grounded one through the right side, moving Robinson to third. Trouble. Hodges came out to talk. On the video, you can see Tom agreeing with whatever Gil had to say. Tom had to have been pitching on fumes; Gil may just have gone out to give Tom a breather.

I recently telephoned Seaver, wanting to know what was on his mind at that moment. Now he's a Napa Valley grape farmer whose vineyard produces a big round complex cabernet under his own label, GTS. Tom had Lyme disease from a deer-tick bite when he'd lived in Connecticut. It's stolen some of his memories. He told me he has no recall at all of himself as the pitcher in that game. I asked Tom if that bothered him. He said, "Yeah." Stupid question.

And now the tipping point: Brooks Robinson versus Tom Seaver. Brooksie had been at the game longer than Tom, but each man had become the face of his team, their town's beau ideal of a baseball hero, Baltimore's quietly excellent professional and New York's exciting new kid on the block. From my spot in medium right, I see Seaver, standing in the cool autumnal sunlight, looking in on Robinson and Grote and umpire Shag Crawford in the grandstand's deep shade. From the stretch, Seaver delivers the ball down and away, a good pitch. But Robinson, who hasn't hit the ball out of the infield all day, squared it up and shot a rope to right center.

Nine times out of ten during the regular season, that ball finds grass. The tenth time comes in a September pennant race, and maybe in a game between divisional rivals, and occasionally if the outfielder is trying to impress a scout or a lady friend in the stands. This time I saw the ball right off the bat and got a tremendous jump.

Into my first couple strides, I'm not sure I'll get there, but it's too late to stop. Sprinting as fast as I can, I'm in that white space where time and thought and sound disappear. I leap; my hat flies off; I have taken the shortest route to intercept the ball, and in free fall I snag that little bastard in the top of my web inches before it finds grass. There's a hush in the stadium, everybody inhaling at once while I'm rolling, skidding, and then I come up throwing, and there's a shriek and a roar like you can't believe, because I made it—made a catch that changed the game, changed the Series, changed my life.

As the poet Robert Browning said, "A man's reach should exceed his grasp, / Or what's a heaven for?" As any Met fan can tell, that moment when my reach equaled my grasp was a little bit of heaven for us all.

Almost from the moment I broke on the ball, I'd been second-guessed. "If the ball gets by him two runs score and we're behind," my teammate Donn Clendenon explained, and if I could ever think as fast as Clendenon, I might agree. But I couldn't do that. Thinking didn't help. Eliminating thinking—that was the point of all those fungos hit by Eddie Yost.

The catch didn't end matters. We hadn't broken but we did bend. First, we still had to get out of the inning, which we did when Elrod Hendricks hit a sharp liner that managed to come right at me for my third putout of the inning.

In the bottom of the ninth, we threatened. With two out and Cleon on first, I singled, my third hit of the game, but then Watt got Shamsky, batting for Charles, to ground out to second. How far did Hodges want to go with Seaver? In today's game, Hodges might have been on his third or fourth reliever by now, but instead, he ran Tom out there for the 10th. Soon Seaver was in another jam. Davey Johnson reached on an error by Wayne Garrett, who had gone in at third for Charles, and then with one out, a pinch-hit single by

Clay Dalrymple put two men on with one out. Like the inning before, a single gives Baltimore the lead. But this time, unlike in Game One, when Don Buford skied one to deep right and it snuck by me for a home run, I came down with it (damn, I had a busy afternoon!), and then Seaver K'ed Paul Blair to end the inning. The bullpen got busy with Ron Taylor and Tug McGraw, the righty-lefty of Hodges's options if he had to pinch hit for Seaver in the bottom of the 10th.

Right-hander Dick Hall took the mound for the O's. Grote led off for us in the bottom of the 10th with a floater to short left center. That was the kind of fly ball we'd been catching the whole Series, but Buford didn't get there, and Grote legged out a double. Sensing opportunity, Hodges immediately sent Rod Gaspar in to run for Grote. Hall then intentionally walked Al Weis to set up the double play. At this point, Gil decided Seaver's day was done. He sent up J.C. Martin to pinch hit.

Like a lot of backup catchers, J.C. earned his spot more for his ability to handle pitchers than his .177 batting average. Hodges could have sent up Kranepool, a professional hitter, but Hodges knew that if the team failed to score and had to go back out for the 11th, he would need Martin to catch.

To counter the Martin move, Earl Weaver brought in Pete Richert, his lefty relief specialist. For six or seven years, Richert had been a hard-throwing starter with the Dodgers and Senators whose record always hovered around .500. The Orioles converted him to a late-inning relief specialist, a role in which he prospered. Today, however, was not his day.

Martin bunted, dropping the ball perfectly about twenty feet in front of the plate on the first base side, too far in for the first baseman Powell to make the play. Richert had to charge off the mound to field it, getting to the ball just ahead of the catcher. His left arm—his throwing arm—is on the first base side, so he has to spin clockwise to put Martin out at first. Except, the throw never reached Davey Johnson, who had come over from second to cover the bag. Richert's throw pings off Martin's left wrist and it caroms into right field. Gaspar, whose foot speed had impressed everyone from the first day of spring training, read the play unfolding in front of him, and scampered home from second with the winning run.

In this age of instant replay, Martin would have been ruled out, I'm sure. A man running to first is required to run in foul territory, to give the fielders a clear lane in which to throw. On the YouTube video, J.C. is clearly in foul territory when he starts to run, but by the time he had gone halfway down the line, he had drifted into fair ground. Looking at a still photo in the next day's paper, Shag Crawford, the home plate umpire in charge of the play, saw Martin's foot on the line and said he still thought Martin was far enough out of the way. The O's had reason to gripe, but baseball is seldom a game that comes down to one play. They could have won the game in the top of the ninth, or the top of the 10th. And even if Richert had thrown Martin out, we would have had men on second and third with one out and Agee coming up. I still like our chances. Bottom line? I've made the catch of my career, my Mets lead the Orioles three games to one, and in less than twenty-four hours we would take the field with Koosman on the mound and a chance to win this damned thing in Shea—the place where we clinched our division, our league, and now had a shot at a World Series champagne party. That would give us a chance to apply the important lesson we had learned in our two previous champagne finishes: Check the labels. Don't be spraying the imported stuff all over one another because what's left to drink is the pedestrian domestic swill. Put the good stuff in your locker and take a bath in the cheap stuff. Get it?

After the game, everybody wanted to ask me about the catch. I knew I had made a helluva play, but there were no videotapes, so I had no objective view. Not until Cecilia and I drove home and watched highlights on the six and eleven o'clock television news did I start thinking, "Goddamn . . . that was an incredible fucking catch." And not until the next day did I sense that this one play might have historical legs. That was when Mickey Mantle, a first-class center fielder in his day, said on the NBC pregame show that my catch was "the best he had ever seen." How do you not want to hear that?

One More

Having now encountered big hits by banjo hitters, a fluky error, and out-of-this-world fielding—not to mention a lot of incredible pitching—the Orioles would still concede nothing. We knew we would still get their best, and indeed, they came out fighting. Top of the third, with Mark Belanger on base, the pitcher Dave McNally smoked one out on Koosman. The two-run home run to start the inning was followed two outs later by a solo monster from Frank Robinson, and just like that we trailed by three. Koosman came back to our dugout livid and announced for all to hear, "Let's get some runs, boys, they will not get another run off me." I had already missed a decent opportunity, striking out with two men on in the first inning.

Baltimore carried the lead into the sixth. But in the top of the inning, their luck began to change. Koosman hit Frank Robinson with a pitch. It was deliberate. "I drilled him for hitting the home run off me," Koosman later wrote. "I hit him right below the cup on his right leg." But although Jerry says he hit Frank, and Frank says Jerry hit Frank, umpire Lou DiMuro ruled the pitch a foul ball.

The pitch apparently rebounded off Robinson's leg and hit his bat, while DiMuro ruled it hit the bat first. Koosman then struck out Robinson with a curveball. In the event Powell had followed with a hit, they could have had two men on, one out, and an overdue Brooks Robinson coming up. Instead, Jerry got the third out, and it was once again our turn.

That's when another break came our way. McNally threw a curveball down and in to Cleon Jones that appeared to hit him on the foot and then bounded into our dugout. Or maybe it came close to hitting him in the foot before bouncing our way. This was back in the pre-sneaker era when we wore black shoes that were freshly polished every day. In what now has become a piece of Mets mythology, Hodges carried the ball out to DiMuro, showed him a shoe polish stain on the ball, at which point the ump said Cleon had been hit by the pitch and awarded him first base. At this point, Earl Weaver threw an epic tantrum, to the point that he got himself thrown out of the game. I couldn't really blame him.

As Koosman later told the writer Peter Golenbock, the ball "came to me [in the dugout]. Hodges told me to brush it against my shoe and I did." That was the ball Gil showed DiMuro. I don't know if that was true, but the whole incident, from wayward pitch to unfavorable ruling to Weaver's argument, possibly cost McNally some focus. Up next came Clendenon, who showed everybody why he deserved the World Series MVP that he would soon take home. He bopped McNally with a two-run shot. The following inning, Al Weis, the mighty mite, also went yard, knotting the game at three. This shit was getting real.

In the bottom of the eighth, Eddie Watt came in to pitch for the O's, and Cleon greeted him with a double off the left field wall. He was the go-ahead run, and after Clendenon grounded out to third, I was due up. I was wondering if Hodges was going to pinch hit Shamsky for me. Sham had hit the Braves hard during the playoffs, but Gil always went with the hot hand and I was hot. Plus I had singled off Watt late in Game Four. I headed for the plate. Nobody was calling me back.

Watt brushed me back with a fastball. My only thought was that I needed to hang tough against the sidearming right-hander. Watt then threw a slider that didn't break quite as much as he might have wanted, and I one-handed it down the left field line.

I have always thought that my ball should have been caught. Don Buford was a hesitant outfielder who chased the ball toward the line and got there just late, in time to backhand the ball on a short hop. Had he dived, I think he would have caught it. Instead Cleon read it well and came around to score, and I stopped at second with a double. There was no fist pumping or hands over my head in triumph—those gestures didn't play back then. But I knew standing there that we had the Birds in hand. This World Championship was ours to lose. That really scared me. It was ours to lose.

It helped that Grote grounded one to the right side and the flip to the pitcher got loose and I came home to give us a two-run bulge. Koozie came out of the dugout and grabbed me right after I scored and the photo of the moment made *Life* magazine. He went out for the ninth and promptly walked Frank Robinson. So, the tying run was at the plate as Boog Powell grounded into a force at second. Brooksie hit a way easier fly ball to me in right and then Davey Johnson floated one out to Cleon that seemed better hit but only made it to the near edge of the warning track. At this writing, I'm looking at the photo of Cleon, signed by him, catching the final out before all hell broke loose on the field.

This celebration was different. It was like the Oklahoma land rush. Fans stampeded out of the stands looking for anything they could get their hands on. Our gloves, our hats, the bases, home plate . . . anything. I grabbed my hat in my right hand and sprinted for our dugout. In one of the wide shots of that moment, you can see me at the right field line, heading in, hat in hand. People's eyes were big as saucers. If you look down the right field line, there's someone leaping onto the field from the high fence where the bullpen guys sat. He's suspended in air, but I can't imagine he didn't break something. Pandemonium reigned on the field at Shea. We headed for the clubhouse and yet another champagne bath. I remember passing Howard Cosell, in the scrum of media waiting outside, and saying something to him like, "You said we couldn't do it, what do you think now?"

In the clubhouse, there was a lot of wet hugging. Eddie Charles pronounced the obvious gloriousness of it all in this Vecsey quote, "This is the summit. We're number one in the world and you just can't get any bigger than this." Our GM, Johnny Murphy, who unbeknownst to us had little more than four months to live, grabbed Hodges and kidded him about Paul Richards's comments that spring in the failed Joe Torre trade about "untouchables and pennants." Here's to you, Paul. The only low note was when Jerry Grote chugged a bottle of vodka and passed out on the floor of the clubhouse wrapped in cold towels, scaring the shit out of us. Among the highlights was seeing Casey Stengel, the spiritual godfather of the whole franchise, hobbling about, enjoying himself. His Youth of America had grown up.

Later that night, we walked to the second-deck seats outside the Diamond Club and saw that the playing field looked like a bombing range dotted with thousands of circles of missing turf. Some of that grass may be still growing in people's yards on Long Island.

Some amazing things happen when your team wins the World Series, and they happen fast. The very next day we went downtown to the studios of Buddha Records and recorded an album that sounded like the sing-along hits of Mitch Miller and his band being tortured by a gang of inebriates, which some of us were thanks to that tableful of champagne. We each got a thousand dollars for singing poorly and getting loaded. After that, we rode through Manhattan's Canyon of Heroes and got showered with ticker tape while millions cheered. On Sunday night, we went on *The Ed Sullivan Show* and lip-synched "You Gotta Have Heart," the cheery anthem from *Damn Yankees* and our freshly recorded album. (Other guests that night included the band Smith, Cyd Charisse, Joan Rivers, the Don Ellis Band, Topo Gigio, and Tanya the Elephant.) Over the winter, it seemed like I appeared at every Little League awards dinner, Sunday morning Holy Name Society breakfast, and Jewish Community Center in the tristate area. In Syosset, they named a little piece of grass "Ron Swoboda Park." I still have the sign, which came down the next day. How fleeting is fame.

I had the chance to join a group of Mets to go to Las Vegas for a couple of weeks and do something that resembled an act, but that would mostly require us to mix with fans and sign autographs. I would have been paid $10,000 for the deal, but I had already committed to making another USO trip to Vietnam. In the midst of the riotous celebration at Shea, I took a phone call from Joey Bishop, the comedian I had met in Saigon the year before. He told me he was taking another group in a couple weeks, and asked me to come along. At that moment, it would have seemed selfish to have told him no. As it turned out, the second trip was even more meaningful than the first. More of the soldiers had heard of me. They seemed more impressed that I was there.

4

Pinstripes

When a team wins the World Series, Major League Baseball gives the players a lump sum, and leaves it to them to decide how to distribute it. Obviously everybody on the roster gets a full share, but usually there are players who were with the club only part of the season. That's why you often hear of teams awarding half shares and quarter shares. I've always been proud of how generous we were, and included the clubhouse guys and groundskeepers in the pot.

Each player on the Mets earned about $19,000 for winning the World Series, a very healthy bonus for all of us. As you might expect, the fellas put the money toward different purposes. Gary Gentry bought a gold-colored Ferrari 330 GT. Jerry Grote and Ken Boswell bought ranches in Texas. Cleon Jones bought a fourteen-foot boat. Tommie Agee just sat on his. The most remarkable investment was shared by Jerry Koosman, Art Shamsky, and Bud Harrelson, who bought a UNIVAC computer. They installed it in an office in Farmingdale, Long Island, and leased it to companies that needed computer services. That was a pretty shrewd deal.

With my share, I bought some land. One of the most special places of my youth was a farm near Annapolis. The place was owned by my great-grandfather Joseph Gomoljak. He grew tobacco and corn, had hogs, made wine, and raised seven handsome kids, three of whom were girls, including my grandmother Agnes. In the one family portrait I own, you can see that she was mighty good-looking. Along with his other enterprises, he kept a still in the woods where he produced liquor that he sold to soldiers stationed nearby at Fort Meade. You won't be surprised to hear that soldiers, liquor, and attractive young women came together in a potent mixture. In fact, Agnes's sister, my Aunt Mary, married a soldier from Fort Meade, who hung around for a while and then took off, never to return. But Aunt Mary took a government job and did fine. Years later, when Joe Gomoljak became an old man, the family started gathering each summer at the farm. I was ten or twelve, and we would have a big picnic, and then we would shoot guns. For me, it became a special place to come to, a hallowed place, full of happy memories.

After the World Series, I began looking for a place where my kids could build some memories. I found a seventy-acre piece of woods near Shawsville, Maryland, that I bought for $19,000, the exact amount of my share. During the rest of my baseball career, the family met there, in groups as large as seventy or so. They came over the All-Star break, in campers and tents. We had a blast.

I still own the land. Over the years, I have done some controlled cuttings of the red, white, and black oak trees to help pay the taxes, but I have never developed the land. My younger son, Brian, and his wife, Charlene, live a short distance from the property, and they adore it. Charlene raised honeybees on the land for one year, until a freeze killed them off; as I write this, I have just finished a jar of their honey. The land is, and will remain beyond my lifetime, a place to come to.

Soon enough it was time to start getting ready for the new year— for the chance to defend our title. At some point in that age before agents, the front office sent me a contract offer for the new season—$37,500. I was disappointed and upset; I had expected more, especially after my second half and postseason contributions.

Unwisely, I let my feelings become public, saying, rather too memorably, that "I would find it impossible to look my wife in the face" if I took that deal. In the end, I did sign the contract, and I have been able to look Cecilia in the face on multiple occasions since then. But I was angry, and anxious, too; I felt I mishandled the situation. There was a lot of ill will, and I had caused it. I was feeling a kind of friction with Gil and with the front office that didn't rise up all the time, but that never entirely disappeared.

The following season, 1970, always feels like the year that got away. We should have done better. We had everybody back, and our youngsters were more experienced. Unfortunately, our 83–79 was seventeen games worse than the shiny 100–62 record we amassed in 1969. We scored 63 more runs than in 1969, but our ERA was up by half a run per game. Maybe we didn't play nearly as well, but the case could be made that we were just plain luckier in 1969 than we were in 1970. The great baseball statistician Bill James uses a formula involving the number of runs a team scores and gives up to predict what its record should be. In 1969, we scored 632 runs and gave up 541, which according to James's formula (which I could not explain to you if you held a gun to my head), should have translated into 93 wins. Instead, we won 100 games. That's what happens when your record in one-run games is 36–23—you get the wins without piling up a big margin of victory. (This goes to show the value of clutch play: that 36–23 record in one-run games got us into first place; the year before, our record in such games was 22–36, nearly an exact reversal, and we placed ninth.)

In 1970, our record in one-run games dropped to a mediocre 24–25. We scored many more runs—695—but gave up many more as well, 630. Still, according to the Bill James formula, that should have been good for 88.9 wins. The Buccos won the division with 89. Maybe we used up our 1970 allotment of good bounces and lucky breaks during the amazing year before.

All of which is a way of saying that we had the division title in our hands, and we let it fall. We spent twenty-five days that summer in first place, juggling the lead with the Pirates and the Cubs. On September 14, we were in first place, but unlike the year before, we staggered to the finish, going 5–10 and winding up in third, six games out. It was ours to lose, and unlike the year before, we did. I hit about the same—nine homers again and a batting average in the .235 range—but I had about 82 fewer at bats, which left me very frustrated. I felt if I played more, I could contribute more; on the other hand, I could have been contributing more with the chances I had, and people were growing impatient. "How can I learn if I don't play every day?" I said one day. "In the minors just like the rest of us," came a voice from the far end. That stung, but like many statements that hurt our pride, there was a lot of truth in it. I was lucky; Ed Kranepool also struggled, and he did get sent to the minors for a spell.

In my disappointment, both in my situation and the team's performance, I stuck my verbal two cents in . . . too many times. Once, after a tough loss in Philly, Gil was speed shaving as per his usual custom, and said something critical to Kranepool. Totally inappropriately, I chimed in with something like, "Well, maybe if you played him more, he'd do better."

Later in the season in Houston, I had dinner with my sister-in-law's mother at a restaurant not far from the hotel where the team was staying. At that time, Houston's liquor laws prohibited restaurants from serving alcohol; if you wanted to drink with dinner, you had to bring your own bottle. Which I did, and which I pretty nearly emptied. I got thoroughly blitzed, and ended up staggering back to our hotel. Somebody—Gil, one of the coaches—saw me in this state. The next day, Gil asked me if I was loaded, and I denied it. He knew I was lying. It was another blow to our relationship.

Come the fall, the same anger that spoiled the last off-season had returned, and if anything, I found it even harder to handle. I groused about Hodges more. I told the front office that I would like to be traded. At one point I said in the paper I didn't think Hodges belonged at the same managerial level as John McGraw, Connie Mack, Joe McCarthy, and Casey Stengel. Given that I was talking about probably the top five managers of all time, I didn't think this would create a controversy, but maybe there was something in the way I said it that caused a flap. Things warmed up briefly once camp opened in 1971. I got a new contract, and everything was hugs and kisses, but even though I apologized for what I said about Gil, I still lobbied for more playing time. That just roiled the waters again, and so about a week before the start of the season, I got the news: the Mets had traded me not just to another team, but to another country. I was now a Montreal Expo.

Any doubt about how far my stock had dropped should have been evident in the terms of the deal: I was traded for Don Hahn, a light-hitting utility infielder. But to complete the deal, the Mets had to throw in Richie Hacker, a minor league shortstop.

Naturally I tried to make the best of it. I put on my new uniform and met the media. "I'm pleased with the switch," I told the media. "It's refreshing to have someone believe in you.

"People think I've been resentful of the Mets, but it's not true. I'm not mad, and I have no regrets. Maybe Gil did want to get me out of his hair. My emotions always have been very close to the surface, and maybe I've used too much flair. But maybe the manager would admit that he'd like to have this kind of enthusiasm from everybody.

"I think maybe people saw more of a human being in me than in others. They saw me do some things right and they saw me fall on my face. But I'm leaving New York with my head high. I did my best and if it's not good enough, why should I be ashamed?"

My new manager, Gene Mauch, was a brilliant baseball man,

and I made sure to say so, but even if I thought he was a dolt I would have said so. I was looking to take playing time from an outfield crew that already included the slugging Rusty Staub, the solid veteran Mack Jones, and the very capable Bob Bailey, all of whom had better stats to show for their recent seasons than I did.

Mauch's teams practiced a different version of baseball from everybody else, featuring a complexity that I couldn't always figure out. I knew I would never be a Mauch kind of player, but I did think I could play for him if he put me in the lineup. But Mauch gave me about the same amount of playing time as Hodges. I played in 39 games, had 75 at bats, good for a .253 average and no home runs. At one point, he suggested sending me down to AAA, ostensibly to work on playing center field. "Why don't you send Boots Day or Clyde Mashore to the minors?" was my response. Within a week, on June 25, I was sent to the Yankees for Ron Woods. The big loser in this deal was the trainer on the Mets, Tom McKenna. I had been renting him our home in Syosset, and now he had to find a new place to live.

The Yankees

When I joined the Yankees in late June, the team wasn't doing so well: 35 wins, 45 losses, good for fifth place, twelve and a half games behind the defending World Champion Orioles. But all was not hopeless. They had some strong starting pitching in the personages of Mel Stottlemyre, Stan Bahnsen, and Fritz Peterson, and some impressive young stars like Bobby Murcer, Thurman Munson, and Roy White. From the point when I joined the club, the team played better, but not well enough. We ended up 82–80, good for fourth place and seats for the playoffs in front of our television sets. I didn't do badly, hitting .261 in 138 plate appearances, with 20 RBIs. That's one run batted in every seven at bats, which would project to a solid 60-plus RBI output for a full-time player. Which I hadn't been for some time, and would never be again.

It's too bad there is no title for practical jokes, because the Yankee teams on which I played would have contended every year. Most of the credit would belong to the left-handed starter Fritz Peterson, one of the rare and aberrant practical jokers alive. He had also been a 20-game winner in 1970, which no doubt earned him a lot of tolerance from management.

Fritz could be depended on for a gag a week. He had some favorite bits that he would pull with regularity. Almost every rookie who joined the club would eventually receive a certificate for a free turkey from Fritz. Printed on very official-looking stationery, a free turkey must have seemed to those usually naive youngsters one of those great perks that come from being a pro. Most of them discovered at their local supermarket that they were the turkeys.

Fritz also worked on building relationships with new players, establishing the kind of rapport where he could casually suggest that the new, young (you didn't pull this shit with veterans) Yankee should go ask shortstop Gene Michael how his sister's dance lessons were coming. It was a setup, of course. Stick would deadpan to the questioner, "You stupid son of a bitch, you know my sister just lost a leg to cancer." Michael would then turn away, and let the poor bastard stew in his rude insensitivity for a couple of days while he tried, in vain, to apologize. Eventually, Stick would let the young guy out of jail and go lie in wait for the next fresh face to prey on. Yes, it's pretty sick.

Peterson was quick to improvise, too. Once outside the hotel in Milwaukee, while some of us were waiting for the bus to the ballpark, a fellow pulled up in front to deliver something to the hotel, leaving his car unlocked. Seeing this, Peterson told a couple of guys it was his car, and if they wanted a ride to the park to just pile in, while he went back into the hotel to get something he forgot. In the meantime, this owner comes back and finds three beefy guys making themselves at home in his vehicle. Peterson was Allen Funt without a camera.

One youngster on the team, Bobby Murcer, would sit in the dugout between innings and rock back and forth. Murcer was a terrific hitter for the Yankees from Oklahoma, which made a lot of people think he would be the next Mickey Mantle in center field. That was unfair; there was only one Mantle, and with a seventeen-year career and 252 homers, people should have been happy that he was the one and only Bobby Murcer. His rocking back and forth was a nervous habit that fans observed on TV. One of them sent Murcer a beautiful wooden rocking chair that sat in front of his locker. Fritz swears he was not responsible for this, but, somebody, and we will never know who, took a hacksaw blade and made little cuts in the joints of that rocker. When Bobby came in and sat down, the thing broke in a bunch of pieces and he went to the floor like a stone. Nobody has ever owned up to it. Maybe because they knew Murcer would have killed them.

Fritz, of course, attained a certain immortality in the sexually restrained world of baseball in 1972 when he and another left-handed pitcher, Mike Kekich, swapped not just wives, but lives. I ran with Kekich a bit on the road; he was a smart guy with a wonderful, free-range hippie brain, and he never held it against me that I got the only hit off him in a one-hitter he threw when he was with the Dodgers in 1968. Fritz, as we've seen, was as inventive as he was mischievous. While some guys were out trying to get laid on the road, Fritz took a scale with him that he could use to weigh the tits of women who might be curious about what their tits weighed. I assume that's all the persuasion that was necessary.

As it happened, Cecilia and I were witnesses to the start of this great moment in the Swinging Seventies. The sportswriter Maury

Allen invited us to a dinner party at his home in Dobbs Ferry, one of the suburbs north of the city. Mike and Susanne and Fritz and Marilyn were also present. What I noticed almost immediately was that Marilyn Peterson was not wearing the full wig that she always wore. Fritz called it her helmet. It was the first time in the two years that I had been with the Yankees that I had ever seen Marilyn's natural hair. As it happened, that would not be the end of the changes Marilyn would be making in her life. We found out later that after the dinner broke up, Marilyn and Susanne switched cars, switched husbands, and switched lives.

Mike's move with Marilyn Peterson quickly hit the skids, and after the season she left him to start another life. On the other hand, Fritz and Susanne Kekich got married and have spent more than forty years together.

The caper with which I am most frequently associated was featured in Sparky Lyle's book, *The Bronx Zoo*. Here's my version. Sparky was an excellent left-handed relief pitcher who would win the Cy Young Award in 1977, and a force of nature besides. One of the things that amused him was to intercept birthday cakes sent to various Yankee players in the clubhouse, myself included. If the cakes were untouched, virginal, if you will, Sparky would grace them with his hairy ass print. One day, a birthday cake was delivered to Sparky, which inspired our third baseman, Graig Nettles, to come up with a disgustingly brilliant brainstorm that would be the ultimate payback. "Who can work up one for Lyle's cake?" Graig asked, whereupon it fell to me to force out a shiny little turd that I laid—handsomely, I thought—on top of Sparky's white birthday cake. Then we closed the box and stuck it back in Sparky's locker. There it stayed for several days with Lyle trying to figure out what smelled so bad. About three days in, Sparky, finally, lifted the lid and "Jesus-God," there it was. We all laughed pretty hard, Sparky included. If it was written by Robert Frost, justice could not be more poetic.

I spent a total of two and a half seasons with the Yankees, during which time I mostly rode the bench for a club that had attached itself to fourth place in the AL East like a barnacle. On September 12, 1973, with two out in the bottom of the seventh in a game we were losing 7–0, I went yard on Roger Moret, a young pitcher who was in the process of winning his eleventh straight game. Two years earlier, almost to the day, also in the seventh inning, I had also homered off Moret, that time to tie a game that we would eventually win. Moret thus became the final member of a small club that included Bill Henry, Steve Carlton, Gaylord Perry, Claude Osteen, and Ron Herbel: major league pitchers off of whom I homered twice. As it turned out, that was my last home run. When the season ended, I knew my time with the Yankees was up.

5

Last Licks

Back then, thirty years old was the tipping point for baseball players. If by then you were not an established starter, if your numbers drifted downward, you were in trouble. I was twenty-nine going on thirty, hitting a robust .116 for the Yankees. In Cleveland, end of the season, cold, raining, eighth or ninth inning, in a game we were running away with, Ralph Houk subbed me in for Matty Alou in right field. For defense? I figured I was out there to keep Matty from getting sick. My unconditional release arrived from George Steinbrenner's office around Christmas 1973, regular mail. I wasn't surprised. I live life as Toynbee described history, "one damned thing after another."

Today, my agent would be online and on his cell looking for a team needing an experienced outfielder. I sat by the phone. The only solid offer came from an old first baseman, Eddie Robinson, general manager of the Atlanta Braves. Their outfield was stacked with Henry Aaron, a home run away from Ruth; speedy Ralph Garr, league leader in triples the next two years; twenty-five-year-old Dusty Baker, an eventual baseball lifer in his prime; and Rowland Office, who would come on for Henry in the late innings of the record game and play eight more years in the National League. The Braves needed one more outfielder. Maybe me?

Eddie Mathews, a tough hombre in anybody's book, managed the Braves. He'd lose the job before the year ended, but four years later he'd carry his 512 homers into Cooperstown. Mathews once mauled and dropped Frank Robinson, nobody's patsy, at third base after Frank cleated him in the head. I hung with starting second baseman Davey Johnson in the Braves camp, a sharp veteran who, it just so happened, made the last out in the '69 series. He told me that the year before he went to fist city with Mathews one night after they both came in with a few drinks in them. Who knows what it was about? Mathews was loaded. Davey is proud he held his own because Mathews could go.

I was desperate to impress. Since my rep was as the guy who made the catch in the '69 Series, I was determined to put leather on anything that came my way. Chasing a fly into foul ground, busting ass, glove almost to the ball, I stumbled on the bullpen mound and splatted into a high-speed facial, coming up with nothing but a mouthful of dirt. In further action, after getting called out on what I viewed as a neck-high fastball, I ranted at the umpire. When I carried the bitching back to the dugout, Mathews turned on me. "Stay off the umps," he shouted. "Shut up." Everyone heard. I fired back, "For chrissakes, I'm trying to make this fucking team." Everybody heard that, too.

The larger issue besides my lousy spring was my $37,500 salary, not what fifth outfielders were paid. At the very end of spring training, exactly when teams are not looking for new players, the Braves snagged Ivan Murrell off waivers. Murrell, in what would be his last year, could play the outfield as well as first base, and wouldn't require as much of ownership's money. I met Mathews in his office. Goodbye.

Before the Braves picked up Murrell, before I got my pink slip, Dave Marash, reporter, anchor, and canny baseball fan at WCBS-TV in New York, had an idea. "I was on my usual springtime mission to find a story that would justify a reporting trip to spring training," Marash says. "I saw that you were going to try out for the Braves. They were loaded in the outfield. Your chances slim. So, I shorted you, bet against you. I went to the news director, Ed Joyce, and proposed a half-hour documentary, *The Last Spring of Ron Swoboda*. And he bought it because you were, even then, an iconic figure in New York City, the lunch-pail guys' favorite blue-collar ballplayer. And, you were, I knew from experience, a great interview.

"Down I went to West Palm where I joined the unique Miami-based team of a blind cameraman and his deaf soundman," Dave says. "Everything went fine for me, so-so for you. The hits weren't falling and the outfielders ahead of you were numerous and talented, and you could read the tea leaves, or was it the fresh squeezed orange pips?"

I was exhausted, stretched out on my bed in the team motel, wearing a T-shirt with a lightning bolt across the front. Dave arrived for his "big interview with a dog-tired, downcast, about-to-be ex-ballplayer."

"Don't move," he said. "We'll do it right here." Unlike my spring training, something magical happened. "You were great," Dave says. "You opened up about your desire to stay in the game, candid about your chances. The conversation didn't play like a standard interview. It was an honest exploration of who you were." Marash filmed Cecilia by herself sitting in our den in Long Island. Unpretentious, unsure of what was coming, she was confident we could handle it together. I'm always running to catch the train. She's in the bar car nursing a Balvenie. Over the interview, Dave's cameraman rolled on Cecilia walking through the greenery in our wooded backyard, dappled sunlight playing off her gorgeous long red hair, a Renoir. Dave put music underneath, Stevie Wonder declaring, "You are the sunshine of my life . . . yeah, and I will always be around you." Like Stevie Wonder wrote it just for Cecilia and me. I would have hired her for something.

Dave edited and screened the half hour. Ed Joyce said, "You know, we need a weekend sports guy. Do you think Ron Swoboda would be interested?"

I didn't have a clue that Joyce was harboring thoughts about me coming to work for him. I was a free agent sitting in the home of a close friend, Harvey Lebow. The bulk of his business was uniforms for girls and boys in Catholic schools in the city. From Harvey's couch, I wondered into a Dewar's, "What the hell am I going to do?" Like an 0-for-5 with five Ks, I had no idea.

The TV was on and I was home alone watching the superstation when Henry broke Ruth's record. In the spring, the stories had been rife about the idiot hate mail sent to Hank. He let it play out. His time came with that unforced, effortless swing. He launched number 715. Tears came. First for Aaron's feat. Greatness with graciousness chokes me up. And I felt bad—I had really, really worked to be there, but I wasn't good enough. While Henry was rolling by Ruth, the game that had made me, the game I loved, was leaving me behind the way I always knew it would. *La fin.*

The notion that professional athletes die twice, once when they can no longer play the game, and again when their hearts stop beating, has been knocked around for a while. At her remove in Baltimore, hearing I'd been released, even Mom said to me, "I feel like somebody died." To paraphrase the Dead Person in *Monty Python and the Holy Grail,* I wasn't dead, yet. I still had a pulse, a large mortgage, two kids, and a wife, all of whom needed me to do something. I'm not big on self-pity. I've been blessed. I'd seen a sign in the crowd at Shea, SWOBODA IS STRONGER THAN DIRT! Just short of my thirtieth birthday, I'd been a contender and played on a World Champion in New York and survived. Don't cue Frank Sinatra here. It's just that transition is scary when you're short of ideas.

The phone rang. WCBS-TV was on the line with an offer of money even-up with what I earned my last year in baseball. Without an agent or any other formality, I said yes. It was easy. Eventually I replaced an experienced, professional sportscaster named John Kennelly, who happened to be working at a Baltimore station during the 1969 series. Kennelly was the author of the funniest line about my famous moment. Reckoning on the improbability of me changing a game with my leather, Kennelly said, "The only way that Swoboda could make a living with his glove, is to cook it and eat it." I felt bad about trumping his wit with my higher Q Score, but what could I do? After my Series catch, and after playing for both New York baseball teams, the viewing audience knew my name and liked my face. I got the job.

Here's the catch. If I tanked on air, they were only obligated to me for thirteen weeks at a stretch. I had no writing skills, no experience editing film or reading copy from a teleprompter. I was a sportscaster on air in the number one television market in the world with nothing more under my belt than four or five diction lessons from a lovely lady who had me reading tongue twisters and repeating "ta-pocketa-pocketa-pocketapocketa." When would I say that on the air unless I was reading from *Walter Mitty*? It was laughable, if painful embarrassment is your idea of funny. I was going to try people's patience. I wasn't even that good of an overall sports fan, and I wasn't that quick of a study. But I needed the gig. As it happened, writing a sports broadcast and then reading it in front of a New York audience was the hardest thing I ever did—for which I have been eternally grateful.

I gravitated toward Marash. Dave was originally a sports guy on the radio. His intelligent bearded look and resonant voice were rerouted into a news anchor chair at WCBS-TV, Channel 2, the Deuce. On the working newsroom set, jacket off, shirt sleeves rolled up, his cigar occasionally entered the frame until better thinking decided that was over-the-top. He and his wife lived up Broadway in the 90s in a spacious apartment. Every wall was shelves crammed with books and vinyl Dave ferreted out of his favorite shops in the neighborhood and along his travels. I was curious, and I was in heaven there. When premier jazz acts hit town, Dave squired me to the Village Vanguard, the Blue Note, or some other club where Dave knew the owner, the musicians, and their music. Later, we repaired to Dave's place and debriefed the evening. Along with music appreciation we might get into art and literature. I probably should have picked his brain more about sports. I could have used the help. He was an education I couldn't have bought. Our friendship is about truth or as close as we can get to it.

The underfinanced World Football League came into being at the same time as my sportscasting career. It was my first assignment. Not that it had been explained to me what television reporters did on assignment. I drove to the New York Stars camp at a high school field. New to conducting interviews, I posed facile questions to the players, including Babe Parilli. He'd starred for Bear Bryant at the University of Kentucky, wore a Super Bowl ring for backing up Joe Namath, and looked happy enough to be there with the Stars, the beginning of his coaching career in the football minor leagues.

We shot cover film of the practice, and I sent the camera crew back to the station. The camera guy might have mentioned something to me about going to the station to write a script. I headed home, happy with my first day's work. I was relaxing on the couch. The phone. Assignments editor. "Where the hell are you? You're supposed to be here writing a script." I was expected to write the story, supervise cutting the film, and create the package I would introduce and close on camera. I was in the news business, all right, and this was news to me.

Then again, everything was news to me. For example, we did not do a *show*. WCBS policy called it a news *broadcast*. I stumbled over copy, pushed deadlines and varying degrees of awfulness to the limit. On one classic broadcast, I thought I'd built a solid, snappy little sports broadcast, using four pieces of highlight film with my narration. I would read my bouncy copy over the footage, and my bosses, who monitored every moment of every broadcast, would stop giving each other those "whose idea was it to hire Swoboda" looks. Unfortunately, the list of highlights I'd given the production desk was out of order with the scripts. None of the highlights matched the stories I introduced. It was a disaster. I have never liked watching myself on camera—which worked against me in baseball because I didn't look at film to improve my hitting—and I didn't review this. I walked to the subway feeling like I just backed over my dog.

In late August I headed back to Queens, not far from my old stomping grounds at Shea. The U.S. Open Tennis Championships were being played. The plan, not all bad, was to do my entire sports segment live from Forest Hills. I was game, highlights and scripts for the six o'clock report all handed in on time in order. I waited by the TV monitor, watching and listening to craggy, square-jawed Jim Jensen, the longtime top-ranked New York anchorman, who had been a decent, helpful guy to me. All would be sweet and peachy. I saw and heard Jim give the lead-in to the sports segment. Off I went, reading the intro to my highlights. I noticed right away that there wasn't any tennis on the monitor. Thinking it was a glitch, I shut it down, quit talking altogether, dead air. But nothing was wrong. My highlights were indeed playing on air. Nobody had informed me that for highlights there wasn't feedback to the reporter from the control room. Another complete fuck-up. That it wasn't entirely my fault made no difference.

There was a different element in pro tennis in 1977. Renée Rich-ards, formerly Dr. Richard Raskind, a forty-two-year-old, six-foot-two transsexual ophthalmologist, had won the right in court to play in the women's draw of the U.S. Open. Richards grew up nearby in Forest Hills, the son of an orthopedic surgeon and a psychiatrist. She'd left her wife and children. Even for New York, that's a lot of story.

The monumental unfamiliarity of it all brought out the inevitable snickers. Someone's smart-ass aside called her the first mixed singles match. I'm sure that when she lunged forward photographers were snapping shots up her skirt. I was courtside at East Orange, New Jersey, the lead-in tournament to the Open. At the most anticipated point in the match, the umpire announced new balls and a titter buzzed through the crowd. Bizarre hardly begins to describe the scene. Beyond the laugh lines, Richards, rangy and forceful, overwhelmed some women. She wasn't quick enough though for the magnificent champions like Chris Evert and Martina Navratilova. The year before, Billie Jean King had beaten Bobby Riggs in the infamous Battle of the Sexes. Here was a whole 'nother wrinkle.

I like the equipment I have down there, my home entertainment center. I guarded it carefully as a professional athlete. You don't have sex change surgery on a whim. This was an intelligent person into middle age, deeply unhappy with the body nature furnished. I interviewed Richards at Forest Hills and found her patient, immensely sensitive, for someone who had jumped through so many hoops to put herself on display. In her autobiography, *No Way Renée,* she regreted the decision to play professional tennis as a woman, as it added more pressure to her new existence than was necessary. Recent internet accounts have Renée counseling Bruce Jenner on his sex change. Nearing my seventy-fifth year, I am eternally grateful for my unambiguous and currently boring heterosexuality.

I lasted four and half years at WCBS-TV. There were bright moments in those twenty thirteen-week contracts. I never, however, got over the feeling that I didn't belong in this building full of competent, driven reporters and anchors. So many people worked so hard to help me succeed. A producer of the late news, Andrew Heyward, a future head of CBS News, spoon-fed me a story that should have won awards. An eye doctor came to the station with evidence that the New York State Athletic Commission routinely ignored eye damage, mainly detached retinas. The commission let boxers back in the ring after bullshit eye checks, again and again. Between my easily distracted nature and the fact that I was too pressed just trying to get out two routine daily sportscasts, I didn't give any justice to the story, which is probably still a problem in the ring.

Jazz pianist Larry Willis composed an instrumental titled after one of my nicknames, "The Rock," short for Rock Head, and I wrote the liner notes for *The Offering*, the album on which it appears. I am a rock head. It takes me time to understand some things, to *get* them. Frustrated by my ignorance or lack of perspective or immaturity, I explode. It's loud, appears violent. As near I can tell without ever having visited a shrink, it's the demanding impatient side of my personality kicking that slow fellow in the ass. Self-directed, short-lived. I frighten people badly who don't know me. Sneak up on me when I'm golfing alone and listen to my conversations with myself, you'd think, "Better get the net, the guy is over the ledge." The thing is, I piss and moan, but I do not quit. That's the deal.

I made too many outbursts in the newsroom. I beat on my typewriter to coax copy onto the page. WCBS aired a story about a man going wacko and shooting up his workplace. I joked from my desk to the newsroom staff, to wit, "When they gas me here, I'm gonna be shootin' some people." Gallows humor, totally. They let me go not long afterward, goons in blue CBS jackets a couple of sizes too small standing by. I couldn't believe they took me seriously. I can understand why. Jim Cusick, the news director for whom I had no respect, called me into his office. He eventually went down the ladder and disappeared. He had a button on his desk that opened and closed the door to his office. Cusick buzzed me and fired me. I arrogantly said, "I'm not sorry I'm getting fired. I'm pissed that *you* get to do it." I should have been embarrassed, but I was too relieved. I bought the whole newsroom champagne, which was served between the early and late broadcasts, and I was done.

Correction: not *done*, just done *there*. I continued to pursue a career in broadcasting, at jobs in Milwaukee and New Orleans, where we settled. Cecilia and I love this city, love its pace, its interests, its enthusiasms, and to find outlets for my own. I've been able to combine my knowledge of sports with my interests in art and history and music and, most of all, my still boundless curiosity to weave together what has been a rich and fortunate life. Although I am still the color commentary on telecasts of the New Orleans Baby Cakes (formerly, the Zephyrs) games—they are the AAA affiliate of the Miami Marlins—and while I work hard at it, it's never felt like work. The rest of my time I spend golfing, reading, and writing this memoir. Cecilia and I have made great friends. This is home, which means this is where we have known love and sorrow, joy, and—sadly, unavoidably—sadness. It was here that I took a call in the early evening of January 5, 2004, New Orleans, in which I learned that Tug McGraw was dead.

We all knew this was coming. The malignant blastomas in Tug's brain had blasted him out of this world, but I was in no way ready for this. Three weeks before I had flown to Baltimore and, with my Mom and Dad, had driven to Philadelphia where the local ALS Association (Lou Gehrig's Disease) was honoring Tug at a luncheon. He was all there, sharp and funny. I loved this guy. Everybody did. How could you not. Tug had a charm that was as natural and organic as his handsome, athletic looks and more. Empathy is a word we use a lot but there's a stronger, wonderfully archaic Old English combination word, fellowfeel, that really describes Tug. He was always in outreach, he wanted to feel people, in a room or in a stadium. It made no difference to him. Walking off the mound after ducking danger before getting the third out, Tug would flap his hand inside the front of his jersey and from that gesture even the guy in Bob Uecker's seats in the back row of the top deck knew Tug's heart was fluttering, too.

Stoicism was a put-on, Tug was real. Even his favorite three lines, not necessarily original, were meant to reveal something intimate that Tug wanted you to know. One was about the first time he had sex being pretty scary. Why? Because it was dark and I was alone. Then, someone asking Tug what he preferred playing on, real grass or AstroTurf? The answer: I don't know, I've never smoked any AstroTurf. And lastly, to the question of what he did with his World Series winner's shares? (Tug was in two: 1969 with me and the Mets and 1980 with the Phillies.) His response: I spent most of it on Irish whiskey and women, the rest I just pissed away. Each line delivered the truth with a wry grin. Now, one of the more powerful and compelling life forces I had ever encountered, in or out of baseball, was gone.

But just as important as the joie de vivre, Tug had integrity—and the nerve to back it up. During spring training in 1970, the town of St. Petersburg, where the team trained, held a dinner in our honor. The governor of Florida, an elderly conservative named Claude Kirk, took the opportunity to politicize the situation, and denounced antiwar protesters as "hecklers in the uniform of the day, disheveled filth and long hair. By golly, they looked like hell and talked like hell." He then pointed to us players. "Just look at their haircuts, and the way they're dressed. By God, they are America the Beautiful. Stand up, Mets!"

Slowly, unhappily, we all got up. Some of us strongly opposed the war, and resented this kind of misrepresentation. But even the more conservative guys resented being used by a politician, and all of us realized we had a relationship with our fans that wasn't based on politics, race, nationality, appearance, or anything but the thrill of baseball.

Then things got worse. M. Donald Grant, the chairman of the board and Mrs. Payson's consigliere, got up and echoed Kirk, calling on everyone to fight against the threat posed by hippies. "These men are representatives of New York and of our country, real he-men!"

The players were embarrassed and angry, but Grant had a lot of influence over management, and nobody wanted to get traded off a defending champion. When it came time for each of us to cross the stage and get an award, most just hurried through the presentation, hoping to get the show over with as quickly as possible.

Not Tug. When he crossed the stage, he offered just about the perfect rejoinder. He held his hand shoulder high and flashed the peace sign.

Afterward, I told him I admired his guts. "If I really had guts," he said, "I'd have held my arm high in the air."

Tug was a Californian, and the first of that breed I had ever met. He showed up one spring day in St. Petersburg, part of a group of talented Met minor leaguers invited to an early camp at Huggins-Stengel Field ahead of the big league guys. The idea was to give Stengel and his coaching staff a look at these guys in the flesh. Along with Tug was his older brother Hank, a legitimate prospect with an unbending, too often self-destructive distrust of authority. He was counterculture to the core.

For a name that seems so common, there were only four players named McGraw, including Tug, who ever made it to the big leagues. We all know John McGraw, the Hall of Fame player with the Baltimore Orioles in the 1890s and later longtime manager of the New York Giants. There was another John McGraw, born in Intercourse, Pennsylvania (always good for a laugh . . .), who pitched one game

for the Brooklyn Tip-Tops in the old Federal League in 1914 and
died in Torrance, California, in 1967. Starting a couple of years later
was Bob McGraw, a right-handed pitcher, who appeared in 168
games between 1917 and 1929 with the Yankees, Dodgers, and Phillies, among others, who also died in California. And that was all.
Hank should have been number five on the list of major league Mc-
Graws but he seemed to turn every disagreement with a manager
or coach into an affront to his intelligence. He was an outfielder and
catcher who could hit; he just couldn't knuckle under to baseball's
reigning sensibilities. Maybe ahead of his time, Hank wouldn't keep
his hair short. He would have fit right in today with the Duck Dy-
nasty beards and hair hats all over the major leagues. Also, Hank
never accepted the black and Latino players being shipped off to different hotels in Florida. I saw it, didn't like it, but didn't make it an
issue because I didn't think I could change it. If Hank thought it
was wrong, at times to his own detriment, he couldn't let it go. Admirable, really. Tug felt the same way, but like me he just didn't
step in front of the bus.

As Tug demonstrated in his biography *Ya Gotta Believe!*, insanity ran in his family. Tug's mother, Mabel, probably would be clas-
sified today as bipolar. When Tug and Hank were growing up, her
condition grew violent and Hank took the brunt of it. Mabel had
to be confined and with her, perhaps, went any faith Hank would
ever have in authority. A younger brother, Dennis, has had trouble
with the law. Tug was, apparently, an aggressive breast-feeder, which
inspired his mother to devise his nickname, the only thing he ever
answered to. His life could so easily have been different.

They called their Dad, Mac. I called him shit. It was all an honest mistake that went like this. In 1965, our rookie year with the
Mets, Mac had a car in Los Angeles. We were all driving from the
hotel to Dodger Stadium in Chavez Ravine. I was trying to get into
the backseat of this two-door coupe, leaning the front seat down,

bending way over to slide in. I thought it was Tug's legs in my way and said, "Hey shit, move over." I looked up, it was Mac in the back. I turned beet red. He got such a kick out of it, from then on, when we got together, Mac's first line to me was always, "Hey, Shit." I loved it. He was one of the guys.

In New York that rookie year, when we were living together and we would go over to Freddy Amarada's place for dinner, we used to love looking at all the memorabilia in Freddy's basement. He had a shrine to the Brooklyn Dodgers, the walls covered with team pictures, individual photos, and newspaper stories from their World Series. Tug turned to me once and said, "Do you think we'll ever be up on somebody's wall like this?" I replied, with a clear lack of prescience, "I don't know." I hadn't even thought about it. Even as rookies, Tug's busy brain saw more in this brave new world we had just entered.

Once when Cecilia came to visit with her sister, Margie, the four of us had drinks at a local neighborhood joint. Tug and I amused ourselves putting out the candle lamp sitting in the middle of the cocktail table by spitting beer in thin streams through our front teeth. Of course, we then became the targets in our little game and then Margie got some until Cecilia said, "Stop it." I'm not sure we appreciated the adult supervision but Cecilia was hard not to listen to.

On a couple of occasions our antics got out of hand, and I ended up injuring Tug. Of course, he could have just as easily injured me, or some completely innocent bystanders. One day Tug came to visit Cecilia and me, while he was still playing for the Mets, and I was working for WCBS-TV. It was winter, and there was snow on the ground. Down the street where we lived in Syosset was a large dry sump. Think of a great big hole with sloping sides that collected water when it rained real hard. The neighborhood kids had a toboggan and they had a nice steep run to the bottom and we thought that we needed to give it a try. Tug was in front as we took off and we two lugs built up some speed and went airborne over a bump at the bottom. I landed on Tug so hard that he sprained his ankle and had to come up with some story to tell the team about slipping on some ice. I think they were putting clauses in the baseball contracts by then where you could break the thing if you did something stupid, like tobogganing down a sump.

Much later, when we were both out of baseball, I injured him again. Tug had gotten active in the Major League Baseball Players Alumni Association, which held golf tournaments in various cities to raise money. Former players would fly in and play golf and sign autographs. I went to a couple of them. Usually Tug would grab the mike at the after-party and just riff. He was incredibly funny, particularly if he had a couple of drinks in him. And if he had more than a couple drinks—well, there were things we didn't talk about with the average fan. Tug was heading down some of these roads, and I'm thinking, "Don't go there, don't go there," but Tug did, pulling it back just short of no-no land. It was funny and brilliant, and I was jealous as hell.

A few more drinks later Tug was crashed in a chair. We were out by the pool in this hotel and Tug's room was on the same level so I got the bright idea that I could throw him over my shoulder, fireman style, and carry him to his bed. Well, a couple of guys helped me stand him up and over my shoulder he went, but two steps into this dance I realized that Tug was heavier than I remember and I wasn't as strong as I thought and over we went backward, landing on my ass and Tug's head. When we finally dragged Tug into his room and onto his bed, he's got this pretty good ding high on his forehead. He was babbling something but he never really came to until the next day. When he did, there was this bright-red abrasion on the left side of his forehead. When I last saw Tug in Philly, three weeks before he passed, I realized the large ugly crescent where they'd gone in after his blastomas was in exactly the same spot. And yes, I always wondered.

There was a Mets event in New York, years after Tug had died, where Tim McGraw, his son, showed up with Faith Hill and I had the chance to walk up to him and thank him for everything he did for Tug after the cancer was found. Tim paid out of pocket for the very best medical care that anyone could get for these cancers that would not be cured. All Tim said to me, almost in passing was, "That's what family does."

Several years before, living in New Orleans, I got a call from Tug asking me if I wanted to drive up to Rayville, Louisiana, where Tim was putting on a big country music concert to help pay for this beautiful new recreational facility he had built for the folks up there and where he had spent most of his teenage years. My older son, Ron Jr., and I hopped in the car and in five hours or so pulled into the compound where Tim and Faith had their buses parked. That evening we were backstage at the country music concert with Tim and Martina McBride before her big voice carried her to the top tier of that business. Faith was into a very difficult pregnancy but still tried to go onstage. She couldn't finish and Tim had to rescue her set, which he did without missing a beat. The next morning Tim and Faith came out of their buses, her without her makeup and still drop-dead gorgeous, the two of them seeming so grounded as a couple amidst the pressures of mega-stardom with two separate careers. Impressive, I don't know how you preserve that, I only hope they can.

I'm writing this in my office looking at Tug's smiling face on the brochure for the ALS luncheon where I last saw him. Pinned onto it is a small snapshot taken by my son from that event in Rayville where Tim is giving Tug a wet willie in his ear. Tim and Tug had forged a wonderful man-to-man relationship even though Tug's recognition of his responsibility for Tim came late in the game.

Without blood checks or lawyers, Tug agreed to meet with Tim, who was coming out of high school and needed help with college. They met for the first time in the lobby of a hotel. When Tug saw his spitting image walk in, that was that. Later, in New Orleans they met again when Tim told Tug he was selling his car and everything else he owned, leaving college and going all-in on a career in country music in Nashville. Tug advised against leaving school but, then, you know how that all came out.

Cecilia and I were in New York City at a 1969 Mets reunion when Tug rounded up a bunch of us and over we went to watch Tim and his band in their first appearance on the Johnny Carson show. Tim had a coolness and sparkle onstage that made what he accomplished in country music and in several movie roles no surprise. I know where a good bit of it came from. What I'm trying to say here, the poet Langston Hughes really said best in his famous lament:

I loved my friend
He went away from me

Unbreakable Bonds

We were black and white, conservative and liberal, but we got along as a team. Considering the incredible social, economic, and political upheaval that defined 1969, that is saying something. Our neurobiological underpinnings scatter us across the behavior landscape like a deck of cards in deft hands, but it is possible for people to come together. In the case of the Mets, the bond between us was baseball, and we played to the best of our ability. Understanding that was what connected us; having the ultimate success has only heightened the bonds between us, and the respect we've always paid to one another.

There will always be a clubby kind of connection between guys who have played major league baseball. Having shared the intensity of the highs and lows, grasping the daily grind of this so-called kids game can only be truly understood from the inside. The connection gets closer amongst people whose careers overlapped in a common era. It's even closer between guys who played on the same team whether you accomplished anything or not. The most intimate connection for me, the reason these words are being committed to paper, is having played on a team that won it all in New York with the Mets in 1969. Those relationships, cemented over our single season in the sun, have been the most enduring and will endure for the rest of our days.

Eventually, it gets personal. My closest connection was with Tug McGraw. We were rookies together, and once joined, I cared about him and what was going on in his life long after we laid aside the balls and bats. The same with Ed Kranepool, with whom I roomed and ran around together in the city and on the road. Eddie has a busy brain, loves business, and has always been an entrepreneur. I also had a special affection for Tommie Agee and Cleon Jones, two men from Mobile who sure knew their way around steamed and boiled crabs.

I've been fortunate that I've been able to keep up with my teammates pretty well. For years the Equitable Insurance Company sponsored a series of Old Timers' Games at many stadiums, and I was lucky to have been invited to a number of them at Shea, and some at Yankee Stadium as well. For more than twenty years, I was also invited to Hollywood, Florida, as part of an annual fund-raiser for the Joe DiMaggio Children's Hospital. A wonderful guy named Joe Reilly was in charge of fund-raising for Memorial Hospital there, and even after Joe passed away, Reilly invited a long list of former major leaguers, including me and a bunch of my old Mets teammates. So, we former '69 Mets didn't lack for chances to see one another a couple of times a year, at least on someone else's dime.

As we approached the 25th Anniversary of 1969, Art Shamsky, with a couple of lawyer friends, created a logo, some salable products, and a series of autographing appearances that brought everyone together for several events around the city. Art included the surviving coaching staff and Mrs. Gil Hodges and all the living players in the project. Sham put together another similar but smaller series of events for the 40th Anniversary.

In terms of gathering together, though, nothing was bigger than when they closed Shea Stadium. The Mets invited a huge roster of former players, our wives and families. My two sons, RJ and Brian, had spent a good deal of their childhood running around in the stands at Shea. When they offered for sale a couple of seats from Shea, I made sure I bought a pair for both boys. Funny, when they renovated the old, original Yankee Stadium, I was offered a couple of seats, free of charge. I gave mine to Don Criqui, the sportscaster, who happened to be standing outside Yankee Stadium. At the time, I just had no place for them, so it was Criqui's good fortune. Don't know what they would be worth today.

Now, as we close in on the 50th Anniversary of 1969, my sense is that individual paid autographing gigs have slowed down. The Mets still invite me to their Fantasy Camp; along with Duffy Dyer, we are the old-timers amongst what is becoming a younger group of former Mets who help out as coaches and managers of the Fantasy Teams. The Mets used to, but no longer do an annual Old Timers' Game at Citi Field, their current home. But I'm happy to say I still get included in an event or so every year. I was invited with Ed Charles to throw out the first pitch in the opening series with the L.A. Dodgers for the National League Championship a couple of years ago.

It's a comfortable thing for me to come back to Citi Field once in a while. The amazing restaurant in left field is run by Tracy and Drew Nieporent of the Myriad Restaurant Group. I met Tracy at a Mets Fantasy Camp a long time ago and our friendship has endured. He is a terrific Mets fan and we've watched a few innings of Mets baseball together in his place in Citi Field, the air full of baseball talk. Drew is a die-hard Yankee fan, but we try not to hold that against him.

There have always been a goodly number of memorabilia entrepreneurs who occasionally call you for dates where you can sit around with your old Mets teamies plus some other former players while signing all sorts of photos, bats, balls, helmets, and such. And while you're doing this you can visit with or just sit and listen to guys you played with.

One of the most memorable conversations I can recall is listening to Tom Seaver and Jerry Koosman, our dual aces with the '69 Mets, talking about how many pitches they could throw in one game before they started feeling gassed out. The reason for the discussion was a game the night before on August 22, in the first season at Citi Field, 2009, when Tim Redding, pitching for the Mets in his last season in the big leagues, had started against the Phillies. Tim had a 1–0 lead after five innings, giving up only one hit with 81 pitches, when he took himself out of the game, turned it over to the bullpen, who promptly turned it over to the Phillies, who won 4–1. Redding was stretched out enough to go 95 pitches, no problem. We didn't spend a whole lot of time putting the bit on current players, which was an old-fartish thing to do. But Seaver and Koosman were completely aghast that anybody would leave a game they were leading with a one-hitter going after five innings and 81 pitches. The consensus between Seaver and Koosman was somewhere around 130 or 140 pitches they started to feel like their stuff was backing up. Redding today coaches in the Washington Nationals minor league system, where the norm is to baby young arms, some of which have already undergone Tommy John elbow surgery in college.

Al Jackson, one of my favorite former teammates, was a starting pitcher in the major leagues when anything short of nine innings was a failure. As a longtime pitching coach in the major leagues after his career, he's seen what's considered a quality start diminish, like the value of a dollar, over the years to the point where 100 pitches is, in most cases, the ceiling for starters. Alvin once regaled my younger son at the closing of Shea, telling Brian that, if he wanted to, he could get Jesus Christ to hit a ground ball. (Jesus Alou might have been a different story.) My son, a knowledgeable baseball fan, has never forgotten that night with Jackson or the easiness of the conversation.

The Baseball Wives Reunion

June 24–26, 2011, was just another weekend of Major League Baseball in Arlington, Texas. But, while the New York Mets were manhandling the Texas Rangers, taking two out of three in an interleague series, there was a gathering of women, sixteen strong. They were, in 1969, for the most part, the young wives of a bunch of New York Mets players who would live the dream and be venerated the rest of their lives for notching the franchise's first ever World Series Championship. As far as I know, no one had yet celebrated these women who were the backbone, the glue that held marriages and families together back then, while their men went in quest of the golden ring. So, for no other reason than the fact that it was long overdue, these women decided to celebrate themselves. By all accounts it was wondrous.

The germ of this splendid idea appeared at a Mets event in New York for the closing of Shea Stadium. My wife, Cecilia, Nolan Ryan's wife, Ruth, and Tom Seaver's wife, Nancy, kicked around the notion of a wives reunion, "a first wives club," said with a smile. That's where it sat for several years until it finally sprang some roots and blossomed. Cecilia and Ruth got the ball rolling on the internet in search of those wives and former wives, some of them widows whose lives had moved in so many different and interesting directions. In line with the national average, half of these women were unmarried to the players of '69. Ruth's husband, Nolan Ryan, now back consulting with the Houston Astros, was then associated with the Texas Rangers, which was where they lived, so Ruth's thinking was, "Dallas was in the middle of the country," and her message to the wives and former wives was, "You just get here and I'll take care of the rest." So, it was Ruth who built the itinerary, and a fair number of the wives and former wives came.

The weekend kicked off Friday night with on-field introductions at the Rangers-Mets game, Saturday featured a luncheon at Neiman Marcus with makeup demos followed by a visit to the Cowboys Hall of Fame Museum, with dinner at J. Garcia's and, later, line dancing at Billy Bob's Texas restaurant watching other people ride the mechanical bull and more. Whew. As hostess, Ruth clearly outdid herself in thoughtfulness and generosity. In my conversations with some of these women, they were clearly dazzled, but what seemed to fill their hearts the most and would, likely, live there the longest were the memories, shared and rekindled, times both terrifying and delightful, being young women thrust into lives in the bright lights and big city that none of them were prepared for. Nancy Seaver talked about being a brand-new wife coming from California in 1967, renting a garden apartment in Flushing, New York, from a peculiar older lady, "a woman with painted-on eyebrows," who was always creeping around the place like Bette Davis in *What Ever Happened to Baby Jane?* Where they showered in a bathtub "with a wraparound plastic curtain" like Anthony Perkins wrapped Janet Leigh's body in in *Psycho.* So that when Tom went on the road, a slightly panicked Nancy checked into the Travelers Motel, across from LaGuardia Airport, and "cried a lot." Ruth Ryan's parents had lived on Staten Island before moving to Alvin, Texas, but none of that experience helped Ruth much when she came to New York as "an eighteen-, nineteen-year-old bride, a baby. When I think about what we did hanging around airports at 3 a.m., driving old cars." That's a reference to a used car Nolan had bought with windshield wipers that only failed in the rain. Sharon Bailey (first wife of Jerry Grote, who started at catcher for the 1969 Mets), who lives joyfully wrapped in her Christianity with the same embrace around her three children and seven grandkids, having grown up in a more rural Texas, found coming to New York back then like a crash course in culture shock 101. "I never really traveled much," Sharon related to me on the phone. "I expected everything to be Texas all over until I went shopping and smiled at someone and they didn't smile back." Sharon and Cecilia became close and still are. Cecilia continued the thought. "We were air-dropped into the city where we didn't know anybody and didn't know anything about it. Most of us with young children, if one of them got sick, you called another wife to help." I mentioned before how Sharon and Cecilia would caravan up from Florida when spring training ended, stuffing their vehicles with kids, and dogs, and everything else. Sharon recalled one trip north, driving in the lead car she noticed that Cecilia had dropped out of sight behind. Heading back she found Cecilia pulled over in the front seat cleaning up our oldest son and the station wagon. As Cecilia continued, "Chipper [our oldest son's early nickname] had an ear infection and had just eaten a hot dog and washed it down with grape juice and I was covered in grape-colored hot dog stuff from his projectile vomiting." It was an adventure, which my friend the New York poet and writer Joel Oppenheimer once defined as, "Something that really shouldn't happen to you." Randy Gallo (Art Shamsky's first wife) nailed it: "We learned to become independent women, to count on each other, to count on yourself. You guys got to be young, we had to learn to be adults."

Randy was all over it. Us guys, young professional baseball players, had married the game before we exchanged rings with the women in our lives. It was a game that monopolized our total beings in such a way that, even when we were home, which was half the time during the season, we were so engrossed in THE GAME, we were mentally somewhere else. On the road, we boarded the team bus, boarded the team flight, bused to the team's hotel, bused to the ballpark, and did it all over again, while our wives took care of everything else, by themselves. That half of these marriages worked now seems like more of a miracle than what we did on the field in 1969.

So, they came, these amazing women. Ruth and Randy Gallo, with a master's degree in clinical counseling, dealing with substance abuse, who still works as a national clinical director. Nadine Jackson, still married to left-handed pitcher Alvin Jackson who suffered a debilitating stroke several years ago. Nadine raised two terrific sons and retired as a teacher. Janet Gentry, now a fiber artist, who's held her family together after her husband, pitcher Gary Gentry, walked out on his marriage and children years ago and has never looked back. Peggy Koonce, wife of pitcher Cal, who passed in 1993 of cancer. Sylvia Cardwell, whose husband, Don, one of the veteran pitchers for us in 1969, passed away several years ago from Pick's disease, a raging form of Alzheimer's on steroids. Phyllis Emminger (Tug McGraw's first wife, long divorced before Tug died of his malignant brain tumor). Yvonne Bennett (first wife of shortstop Bud Harrelson, who has the opening stages of Alzheimer's). Carole Cohen, Ed Kranepool's first wife. Eddie, long diabetic, at seventy-four, in search of a new kidney. There was Lynn Dyer, still married to Duffy, a backup catcher in '69. Lyn McAndrew, still married to right-handed pitcher Jim, who came through an emergency prostatectomy with flying colors. And LaVonne (Koosman), no longer married to Jerry, one great left-handed pitcher who still trolls me with right-wing stuff on the internet. The one exception to the rule was Pam Frisella. Her late husband, pitcher Dan Frisella, appeared in exactly three games for the 1969 Mets, all of 4.2 innings of work in relief. Pam married Dan a year and a half after 1969, then lost this fine man in a dune buggy accident in 1977. The end of his life and a very decent major league career at the age of thirty. Pam, who's never remarried, has done many other things, including serving eight years on the town council in Foster City, California and two one-year terms as mayor, and has stayed friends and in touch with Ruth. So while technically not a '69 Met wife, she lived the life, knew a bunch of the other women, and for that she belongs.

Not every '69 Met wife was interested in the reunion. Melanie Pfeil, married and divorced from Bobby Pfeil, a utility infielder, for her own reasons said no thank you. Initially another nonattendee was Nancy Seaver, who now is the boss of the vineyard in Calistoga, California, since Lyme disease had started stealing Tom's priceless memories. It was around 2011 that Nancy lost her Dad, and at first blush thought she wouldn't come to Dallas, but "I got to talking with my [three] brothers and they thought the trip might be good to get me out of where I was in the grieving process." Nancy's brothers were right. "The minute I stepped off the plane I flowed right back into a comfort level." Randy Gallo, again: "I was struck by, after all those years, not really keeping in touch, I was so comfortable we were together. Everybody was so familiar." Ruth, who spent the most time of anyone as a baseball wife, and looked so comfortable in the front row on TV at the Astros playoffs games in 2018, says, "I remember those times [with the Mets] and those years better than all the other twenty-six" years that Nolan played Major League Baseball—twenty-seven if you count the two games he appeared in for the Mets in 1966.

So, you can imagine everyone exchanging albums full of photos of kids and grandkids, the conversations on families finally working their way around to the cynosure of 1969, the World Series that opened in Baltimore. In Major League Baseball, the players' wives have always been striking women, well-dressed, creating a presence at any game they attended. Our wives stepped it up after we lost the opener. LaVonne (then Koosman) related this story. After the first game, the wives noticed a lack of Met banners around the ballpark. To correct that LaVonne and Lynn Dyer got their hands on a black Magic Marker and stole a bedsheet from LaVonne's room, laying it on the floor where they wrote a large LET'S GO METS. "When we lifted it off the floor an imprint of Let's Go Mets was also left on the carpet." Oh, well. Then, LaVonne, Lynn Dyer, Ruth Ryan, Melanie Pfeil, and Nancy Seaver paraded their sign between innings in the hostile confines of Baltimore's Memorial Stadium. From LaVonne: "Pretty brave ladies, to say the least." We won that game, so the banner worked. After clinching at Shea, everybody, players, wives, and Mets staff, went upstairs to the Diamond Club to party. Ruth Ryan remembers her first-time romance with too much champagne. "I had a three-day hangover."

Ruth Ryan, so welcoming and warm, the hostess with the mostest, a woman at ease with herself as wife of Hall of Famer Nolan Ryan and mother of a daughter and two young men who both work in professional baseball. Ruth, who has never lost touch with her roots in Tyler, Texas, said to me on the phone, "There was no more meaningful group I was ever with than these '69 wives." Randy Gallo, whom we would see occasionally when her job brought her to New Orleans where Cecilia and I live, spoke of the joy, rare for her, "to be with people who you didn't have to explain anything to about your youth."

So, here's to these women, strong and resilient, these women who handled so much, so well when they were so young. And here's to what they've become. Truly amazing, a word that's become almost hackneyed in its overuse in reference to the 1969 World Champion Mets. Amazing works just fine in describing this special group of women who decided to gather, by themselves, for themselves. A big part of the reward for Ruth Ryan, who did so much to organize the perfect weekend, came in the mail. "I got some of the sweetest letters and cards. Occasionally, I take them out and read them." Cecilia could hardly speak about the gathering in Dallas without the emotion catching in her throat. They shared so much, so many stories that haven't been told, stories that really belong to these special women. And that's just as well.

I'm hoping, too, that understanding all of this a little better is part of my growing up. I'm hoping.

The Games End, the Name Hangs On

It has always tickled me when somebody in a movie or a TV show drops my name or face into the program to create some effect or another. Why wouldn't it? We do love the sound of our own name, even more than Beatles songs or Christmas carols. I'm certainly aware that by playing for both the Mets and the Yankees, and then doing television sports at WCBS-TV for several years, I have acquired a particular New York identity among people of a certain age group. Though I never worked it, I did, always, try to appreciate it. Hell, it's been worth a few accidental bucks over the years, but it was never a source of arrogance (my least favorite word in English) or a license to be a jerk. It's a by-product of a process, nothing more or less. It's still neat, even when it's just a mention.

The first drop-in I was aware of was in a 1966 movie, *Penelope,* in which Natalie Wood plays a rich housewife who decides to rob her husband's bank, where I think she picks up my baseball card and asks, "Who's Ron Swoboda?" I suppose that it didn't hurt that another character, a con woman played by Lila Kedrova, was named Sadaba. About thirty years later, in a New York–based boy-girl sitcom called *Mad About You,* Paul Reiser and Helen Hunt talked about Ed Kranepool and me. Reiser, born in Manhattan in 1956, would have been just the right age to have been a Mets maniac.

In 1999, a bunch of my Mets teammates and I went out to Hollywood and appeared in one of the episodes of *Everybody Loves Raymond.* We had a wonderful time doing it. Ray Romano and the whole cast and producers treated us like kings. I think I learned that people who come out of stand-up comedy seem to have a better appreciation for their success. Peter O'Toole's character in *My Favorite Year* said, "Dying is easy, comedy is hard." Not an original thought but apt. In Art Shamsky's book *The Magnificent Seasons,* Romano tells him that as a twelve-year-old kid he was actually at Shea Stadium when we clinched the division in 1969. Phil Rosenthal, another New York kid and creator/executive producer of the sitcom series, goes even further in Sham's book: "The 1969 Mets were everything to all my friends and me. We lived, breathed and ate the Mets. From the Mets, I developed a kind of hope and possibility in underdogs." That goes to the heart of why, almost fifty years later, "we few, we happy few, we band of brothers," we 1969 NY Mets are such a fortunate bunch.

The episode, in year three of the series, was called "Big Shots," and the theme of comeuppance plays out. If you think you're hot stuff, there's always a bucket of cold water waiting for you. In the episode, we play ourselves during an autographing appearance at the Baseball Hall of Fame in Cooperstown. I had a small speaking part with Tug McGraw, who was grinding Ray's sportswriting character over a snarky piece he wrote on Tug, all the while Ray was trying to jump the line to get an autograph.

The producers paid me as a member of what is now SAG-AFTRA (Screen Actors Guild and American Federation of Television and Radio Artists). It allowed me to become vested in the pension program at age sixty-five. It's a small sum but the episode we were in still plays on cable and online and we get a small residual payment several times a year. Friends and people I run into see it all the time. It's been a gift that keeps on giving. Thank you Phil and Ray.

In the year 2000, I got a call from someone in Los Angeles whose name escapes me. There was a movie being made, and the plan was that I would appear in it for just a flash in my Mets uniform on deck and mention my name a couple of times. Though they didn't have to, they sent me a check for like $200. The movie was *Frequency,* starring Dennis Quaid and Jim Caviezel as a father and son who connect through the magic of an atmospheric anomaly and an old shortwave radio. This allows the son, Caviezel, to make a leap in time and talk to his father, a fireman played by Quaid who was killed in the line of duty. Without either of them understanding who's who and when's when over the radio, the talk turns to the 1969 Mets and my name pops up. The son says, "Man, I'll love Ron Swoboda till the day I die."

Later, when the movie, a pretty decent effort by the way, cycled to videotape, I got a call from Steven Scavelli, president and owner of Flash Distributors, who was marketing the VHS videos in the NYC area. Steven had a sales contest for his people, the culmination of which would be a dinner in Manhattan featuring the movie's writer, Toby Emmerich, and yours truly. Emmerich, as I came to find out, is not a New York guy and knew nothing about the New York Mets. All of which made me even more curious about how and why he chose me to feature in his film in such a way. It seems Toby did his research in the microfilm libraries of the New York newspapers; from their accounts, he deduced that I came across as an Everyman. I thought that was very cool, since that was all I was ever shooting for. I was this person who happened to play baseball, who happened to be questioned by sportswriters, and, from my point of view, just tried to tell the truth. Toby Emmerich extracted something authentic and human from the newspaper accounts of my ups and downs and wrote me into his film and I got a wonderful trip to New York City that I've never forgotten.

I remember, vividly, watching *Frequency* with Cecilia at a theater here in New Orleans, anonymous in the dark, and when the scene pops up in a flashback with me on deck in Shea Stadium and they deliver the line about always loving Ron Swoboda, I was thinking, should I yell out loud, "I'm that guy!"? Of course, I would not.

In 2008, Robert De Niro and Al Pacino played a couple of NYPD detectives in a flick called *Righteous Kill*. They're talking and the name "Swoboda" appears. I think they were referencing glasnost or perestroika, the beginning of the end of communism in Russia in the 1980s, and the word "svoboda," which means freedom in Russian, came out. But one of them said "Swoboda" and the other one went, "Ron?" . . . and that was that.

The last time my name came bubbling up in somebody's script was in the cartoon sitcom *The Simpsons* when Homer Simpson, TV's most satirically sagacious lout, in the context of baseball, was having a discussion with his wife, Marge, who declared, "Fly balls and fungos come and go, but families are forever." To which Homer blathers back, "I've got to call bullcrap on that. The '69 Mets will live forever, but you think anyone cares about Ron Swoboda's wife and kids? Not me, and, I assume, not Ron Swoboda." Matt

Groening created this wonderfully blunt series that rolls over political correctness like a big highway compactor on a gravel road. I may have taken a hit here but I love what they do with *The Simpsons*. There's a time for politeness, but political correctness gets in the way of the truth. Right on, Homer.

Epilogue: Reflecting on a Miracle

In my Dad's club basement in Baltimore, there hung a framed color lithograph of a Norman Rockwell painting depicting Brooks Robinson signing autographs for his fans. Dad paid fifty bucks for it at an Aberdeen, Maryland, department store where Brooks was making an appearance. Robinson had bought the original painting and its copyrights for a couple hundred thousand dollars at a Sotheby's art auction, and had prints made from it. Brooksie inscribed it, "To John Swoboda, Father of Ron, who I made 'famous.'—Brooks Robinson, Hall of Fame 1983." It's a true statement, and every time I'm with Brooks, I thank him for not hitting the ball directly at me. Otherwise, it's an ordinary put-out, and I've got nothing. I've often said, "If you play nine years in the big leagues you should leave with at least ten seconds of highlight footage." I just made it.

Sports thrives on upsets. We love winners and we love dynasties, but the truth is, everyone who plays sports at a high level is a gifted athlete who has known success at many levels. And the truth is, sports are designed to produce winners. *Somebody* is going to win the World Series this year. *Somebody* is going to win the Super Bowl. And *somebody* is going to win the one after that. But the upset—the surprising victory of the underdog—that's something sweet.

During my life, there have only been two upsets that have captured the public's imagination: the victories of the 1969 Mets and of the 1980 U.S. Men's Olympic Hockey team. In both cases, the victory was beyond the ordinary win by an average underdog; the truth is, no one with an ounce of knowledge would have bet a dime on our chances. But what's more remarkable, both of these wins came at times of great public upheaval, when people had lost confidence not just in their institutions, but also in the future. It's not that people felt that catastrophe was coming; it was more like they thought a losing streak had settled in, and no one saw a way out. And what both those teams managed to do was restore a sense of confidence. If I heard it once, I heard it a thousand times, "If the Mets can win the World Series . . ." Every one finished the sentence in his or her own way. We made it seem like thousands of things were possible, because the event gave thousands of people hope.

It was the privilege of my life to have played a part in the Saga of the Amazing Mets. I wonder if I had been a better player whether the story would have been the same. If I had been a great hitter during my whole career, then my .400 average during the Series would have been just another good job by another good player in the long annals of great players. And if I had been a slick fielder during my career, then I would have just been doing my job. But I was an inconsistent hero and a mistake-prone fielder, and the fact that I managed to come through at the right moment—just like Al Weis and J.C. Martin and Gary Gentry and Art Shamsky and the other guys managed to come through at their right moments—well, that's what made it amazing. In the movie *Oh, God!*, George Burns, playing the Heavenly Father, jokes "The last miracle I performed was the '69 Mets. Before that, it was parting the Red Sea." That's what I mean—there is a World Series champion every year, but there hasn't been another miracle in baseball in fifty years.

It's been a blessing to have been a vehicle through which so many people have been able to touch that experience. Years later, people still ask me to sign a baseball card, or want to show me a little bottle in which tufts of grass ripped off the Shea Stadium infield are saved, or who just want to reconnect for a second to that moment of brilliance that meant so much to all of us. I wanted to be a ballplayer. I never anticipated being a hero. But I was in the right place at the right time. The ball went into my glove. The moment chose me.

Entering Citi Field, where the Mets play these days, above the gate, behind box print letters spelling out RIGHTFIELD, is a twice-life-sized black steel silhouette of me in full layout on my backhand, honoring Brooks's sacrifice fly. Or, more aptly, my catch. It's a creation by Corey Mintz, a Met fan to this day, then part of the design team at Two Twelve, a New York City firm. When he presented the idea to the Mets' owners, he suggested generic baseball images, which they thought to be extravagant and expensive. Not until Corey suggested taking the images from Met history did the owners warm to the idea. In the end, they chose three great catches: Tommie Agee's spectacular catch from Game Three; Endy Chavez's amazing leaping grab from the 2006 NLCS; and mine. How sweet is that?

Just think: If Brooks Robinson hits a solid single, maybe we end up talking about the 1969 World Champion Orioles. If Robinson hits an ordinary fly ball, maybe there's really nothing for me to say. But Robinson hits a sinking line drive, and as a result a vestige of me rises high in Flushing. As long as Citi Field stands, fans coming through that entrance will walk under a reminder of my catch, and the story of the Amazing Mets.

As I was finishing this memoir, my Dad passed away. He was ninety-six years old. He did it on his terms. We had organized a ninety-sixth birthday party for him and as hard as everything was for him then, Dad got up for it and let us celebrate with him. After that, he stopped taking his medications and decided to let nature take her course. Less than two months later, on April 22, I got a call from Franklin General Hospital, where he had been taken. They told me his pulse was failing and that he was comfortable, quiet, and clean, but this was the end. And so it was. But I couldn't help admiring how my Dad had pulled it off. Knowing that he went when he was ready to go will be a comfort forever.

My Mom died of cancer in April of 2006. She wanted so much to live and fought it all the way. When the doctor told her there was nothing further they could do for her, she said the most painful thing I ever heard, "I don't want to die." I know exactly how she felt. At seventy-four years old, with my wife, Cecilia, in strong recovery from her cancer surgery the previous year, I am as happy and fulfilled as I could imagine being at this age. So many wonderful friends, so many wonderful things have entered my life, none of which I felt like I had coming. My heart is full of joy.

In the season before the Amazing Mets had their moment of glory, Robert Lipsyte of *The New York Times* wrote a column called "I Am Swoboda." The piece took the form of the observations of a friend who said that he identified with me. "I've tried very hard to be Fran Tarkenton or even Joe Willie Namath," the man said, name-checking the two future Hall of Famers who were quarterbacking New York's two NFL teams at the time, "but I don't even know how far they draw back their arms to pass. Some friends of mine skated in private school in Massachusetts, and they can be Boom Boom Geoffrion"—the great hockey goal scorer who was then winding up his career with the New York Rangers—"but not me. And who's that fellow who plays goal for the soccer team in New York? I don't even know what the ball feels like. But I am Swoboda."

I'll take that. I've known failure and success, embarrassment and acclaim. More importantly, I've known love every day of my life. And purely by the whim of fate, I was able to make a catch that helped make a miracle that gave joy and hope to millions.

I am Swoboda!

And I am a lucky man.

Index